50 WALKS IN
Dorset

50 Walks in Dorset

Published by AA Publishing (a trading name of AA Media Limited, whose registered office is Fanum House, Basing View, Basingstoke, Hampshire RG21 4EA; registered number 06112600)

© AA Media Limited 2019
First published 2001
Second edition 2008
Third edition 2013
This edition 2019

Field checked and updated by
Dixe Wills

Mapping in this book is derived from the following products:
OS Landranger 183 (walks 1-2, 7-9)
OS Landranger 184 (walks 4-6)
OS Landranger 193 (walks 22-23, 33-35)
OS Landranger 194 (walks 10, 13-15, 19-21, 24-28, 31-32, 36-37, 42-45, 50)
OS Landranger 195 (walks 11-12, 16-18, 29-30, 38-41, 46-49)
OS Explorer 118 (walk 3)

© Crown copyright and database rights 2019 Ordnance Survey. 100021153.

ISBN: 978-0-7495-8118-3
ISBN (SS): 978-0-7495-7438-3

A CIP catalogue record for this book is available from the British Library.

Series management: Donna Wood
Editor: Liz Jones
Designer: Tom Whitlock
Digital imaging & repro: Ian Little
Cartography provided by the Mapping Services Department of AA Publishing

Printed and bound in Italy by
Printer Trento SrL

A05661

We would like to thank the following photographers, companies and picture libraries for their assistance in the preparation of this book. Abbreviations for the picture credits are as follows: Alamy = Alamy Stock Photo
12–13 funkyfood London - Paul Williams/Alamy; 23 Avalon/Photoshot License/Alamy; 33 Colin Varndell/Alamy; 49 John Snowdon/Alamy; 71 Dave Jory/Alamy; 93 Purple Pilchards/Alamy; 109 Greg Balfour Evans/Alamy; 119 Stuart Black/Alamy; 129 Graham Hunt/Alamy; 139 Dave Porter/Alamy; 149 Anthony Wiles/Alamy; 159 robertharding/Alamy; 169 Andrew Ray/Alamy

The contents of this book are believed correct at the time of printing. Nevertheless, the publishers cannot be held responsible for any errors or omissions or for changes in the details given in this book or for the consequences of any reliance on the information it provides. This does not affect your statutory rights. We have tried to ensure accuracy in this book, but things do change and we would be grateful if readers would advise us of any inaccuracies they may encounter by emailing walks@theaa.com.

We have done our best to make sure that these walks are safe and achievable by walkers with a basic level of fitness. However, we can accept no responsibility for any loss or injury incurred while following the walks. Advice on walking safely can be found on pages 10–11.

Some of the walks may appear in other AA books and publications.

Visit AA Publishing at theAA.com

AA

50 WALKS IN
Dorset

CONTENTS

The walks

HOW TO USE THIS BOOK

Each walk starts with an information panel giving all the information you will need about the walk at a glance, including its relative difficulty, distance and total amount of ascent. Difficulty levels and gradients are as follows:

Difficulty of walk

● Easy

● Intermediate

● Hard

Gradient

▲ Some slopes

▲▲ Some steep slopes

▲▲▲ Several very steep slopes

Maps

Every walk has its own route map. We also suggest a relevant AA or Ordnance Survey map to take with you, allowing you to view the area in more detail. The time suggested is the minimum for reasonably fit walkers and doesn't allow for stops.

Route map legend

--->--	Walk route	▢	Built-up area
❶	Route waypoint	▢	Woodland area
— — —	Adjoining path	🚻	Toilet
•	Place of interest	🅿	Car park
⌂	Steep section	⊞	Picnic area
⧵⫫⁄	Viewpoint	)(	Bridge

Start points

The start of each walk is given as a six-figure grid reference prefixed by two letters referring to a 100km square of the National Grid. More information on grid references can be found on most OS and AA Walker's Maps.

Dogs

We have tried to give dog owners useful advice about how dog friendly each walk is. Please respect other countryside users. Keep your dog under control, especially around livestock, and obey local bylaws and other dog control notices.

Car parking

Many of the car parks suggested are public, but occasionally you may have to park on the roadside or in a lay-by. Please be considerate about where you leave your car, ensuring that you are not on private property or access roads, and that gates are not blocked and other vehicles can pass safely.

Walks locator map

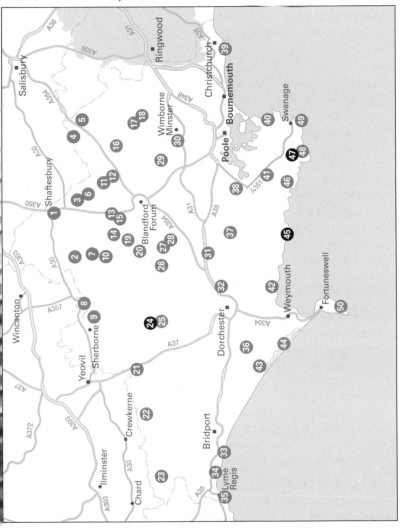

EXPLORING THE AREA

A dark diamond of green velvet on the patchwork quilt of English counties is how many people imagine Dorset. Some will head to seaside Lyme Regis to experience its literary associations and to forage on the cliffsides for fossils.

TAKE YOUR TIME

Be warned: as the good people of Dorset know only too well, there is no point in visiting their county in a hurry. There are no motorways here, and the trunk roads, bold enough on the map, are invariably shared with tractors, tanks, cows and caravans. So relax and slow down. Better still, prepare to leave your car and start exploring on foot, for that's when you'll see the best of the hidden valleys and secretive hamlets that the county has to offer.

And the walking in Dorset is great. With the exception of some of the more spectacular cliffs along the coast, it's rarely strenuous and you're unlikely to get lost for long. There are no vast moorland wastes, scary mountains or devilish quicksands here. Folk have been tramping over Dorset since time immemorial and have left behind them an intricate network of lanes and byways, broad green droving roads and bridleways, which today are very well signposted. You'll find yourself criss-crossing long-distance trails such as the Ridgeway, the Hardy Way, the Monarch's Way and the Liberty Trail. And finding your place on the map is not difficult in a landscape where there's generally a little farmhouse or two somewhere in sight, or a lichened church tower to announce the next village.

CHARACTERFUL TOWNS

With the exception of the unlovely urban spread that is Bournemouth and Poole rolled into one, the towns here are mostly small and full of character. No one who has visited Shaftesbury, Swanage or Dorchester, for example, could fail to be charmed.

In the southwest corner, near the Devon border, lively Lyme Regis is a classic seaside holiday town, its historic heart the familiar backdrop to many a celluloid tale of sailing ships. It offers unrivalled access to Dorset's western coast, with its pretty little villages, its crumbly golden cliffs and the remarkable long shingle strand that is Chesil Beach.

THE DORSET DIAMOND

Shaftesbury, at the northern point of the Dorset diamond, is a bustling market town set on a high hill, the key to the chalky sweep of Cranborne Chase and the fertile flats of the Blackmoor Vale. The roads from here wind gently south towards Wareham and the shallow fingers of Poole Harbour, and southeast to the historic centres of Wimborne Minster and Christchurch.

THOMAS HARDY

Dorchester lies inland from the southern tip of the diamond, an access hub for the green centre of the county, with roads leading south to Weymouth and the Isle of Portland, west to Bridport, north along the lovely Cerne Valley, and east to the white cliffs of the Isle of Purbeck and beyond. The stately town is synonymous with the Victorian novelist and poet Thomas Hardy, who immortalised a still recognisable Dorsetshire landscape.

Wherever you walk, you'll find that the hills, hedgerows and coastline are teeming with deer, birds and other wildlife. It's worth carrying binoculars with you and being prepared to stop and watch patiently – the wildlife will invariably come to you. There are so many great possibilities for walkers all around Dorset that couldn't be crammed in here. Look on this selection as the first 50, and enjoy the further discovery yourself.

PUBLIC TRANSPORT

In a predominantly rural county like Dorset, public transport options are rather limited. With that in mind, all these walks are circular, allowing you to return to a start point and vehicle. For details of public transport services across the county visit Traveline: traveline.info

WALKING IN SAFETY

All these walks are suitable for any reasonably fit person, but less experienced walkers should try the easier walks first. Route-finding is usually straightforward, but you will find that an Ordnance Survey or AA walking map is a useful addition to the route maps and descriptions; recommendations can be found in the information panels.

Risks

Although each walk here has been researched with a view to minimising the risks to the walkers who follow its route, no walk in the countryside can be considered to be completely free from risk. Walking in the outdoors will always require a degree of common sense and judgement to ensure that it is as safe as possible.

- Be particularly careful on cliff paths and in upland terrain, where the consequences of a slip can be very serious.

- Remember to check tidal conditions before walking on the seashore.

- Some sections of route are by, or cross, busy roads. Take care, and remember that traffic is a danger even on minor country lanes.

- Be careful around farmyard machinery and livestock, especially if you have children with you.

- Be aware of the consequences of changes in the weather, and check the forecast before you set out. Carry spare clothing and a torch if you are walking in the winter months. Remember that the weather can change very quickly at any time of the year, and in moorland and heathland areas, mist and fog can make route-finding much harder. Don't set out in these conditions unless you are confident of your navigation skills in poor visibility.

- In summer remember to take account of the heat and sun; wear a hat and carry water.

- On walks away from centres of population you should carry a whistle and survival bag. If you do have an accident that means you require help from the emergency services, make a note of your position as accurately as possible and dial 999.

Countryside Code
Respect other people:

- Consider the local community and other people enjoying the outdoors.

- Co-operate with people at work in the countryside. For example, keep out of the way when farm animals are being gathered or moved, and follow directions from the farmer.

- Don't block gateways, driveways or other paths with your vehicle.

- Leave gates and property as you find them, and follow paths unless wider access is available, such as on open country or registered common land (known as 'open access land').

- Leave machinery and farm animals alone – don't interfere with animals, even if you think they're in distress. Try to alert the farmer instead.

- Use gates, stiles or gaps in field boundaries if you can – climbing over walls, hedges and fences can damage them and increase the risk of farm animals escaping.

- Our heritage matters to all of us – be careful not to disturb ruins and historic sites.

Protect the natural environment:

- Take your litter home. Litter and leftover food don't just spoil the beauty of the countryside; they can be dangerous to wildlife and farm animals. Dropping litter and dumping rubbish are criminal offences.

- Leave no trace of your visit, and take special care not to damage, destroy or remove features such as rocks, plants and trees.

- Keep dogs under effective control, making sure they are not a danger or nuisance to farm animals, horses, wildlife or other people.

- If cattle or horses chase you and your dog, it is safer to let your dog off the lead – don't risk getting hurt by trying to protect it. Your dog will be much safer if you let it run away from a farm animal in these circumstances, and so will you.

- Everyone knows how unpleasant dog mess is and it can cause infections, so always clean up after your dog and get rid of the mess responsibly – bag it and bin it.

- Fires can be as devastating to wildlife and habitats as they are to people and property – so be careful with naked flames and cigarettes at any time of the year.

Enjoy the outdoors:

- Plan ahead and be prepared for natural hazards, changes in weather and other events.

- Wild animals, farm animals and horses can behave unpredictably if you get too close, especially if they're with their young – so give them plenty of space.

- Follow advice and local signs.

For more information visit naturalengland.org.uk/ourwork/enjoying/countrysidecode

SAXON SHAFTESBURY

DISTANCE/TIME	3 miles (4.8km) / 2hrs
ASCENT/GRADIENT	322ft (98m) / ▲
PATHS	Town pavements, steep cobbles, quiet lanes
LANDSCAPE	Town and far-reaching, pastoral views
SUGGESTED MAP	OS Explorer 118 Shaftesbury & Cranborne Chase; tourist information centre has good town-centre maps
START/FINISH	Grid reference: ST862230
DOG FRIENDLINESS	Town centre not good for dogs (lots of road walking)
PARKING	Several car parks around town centre
PUBLIC TOILETS	At car park next to tourist information centre

The town of Shaftesbury is thought to have been founded by the Saxons. The highest town in Dorset, and near to the county border with Wiltshire, Shaftesbury is surrounded by the rolling countryside of the Blackmoor Vale.

In medieval times worshippers flocked to Shaftesbury Abbey. It played a central role in the town's daily life, and Shaftesbury became an important pilgrimage site; the remains of St Edward the Martyr were moved to Shaftesbury Abbey in AD 979. Today, people still come to visit the garden containing the excavated foundations of the original abbey and to visit the Abbey Museum. The walled garden showcases a medieval orchard and also grows more than 100 varieties of herbs.

During the 18th and 19th centuries, Shaftesbury was a centre for button-making. Sadly, the introduction of a mechanical button-making machine to the industry ended the trade's existence in the town and resulted in several hundred families leaving the area, many destitute. However, over the years, coaching inns have continued to thrive in Shaftesbury, benefitting from the town's position on the main route to the West Country, as a stop on the five original main turnpikes (toll roads) in the area.

Tourists stay or come through here to enjoy the quintessential English countryside, but works by iconic authors and film directors have also played their part in attracting tourists; Ridley Scott filmed his nostalgic bread advert here in 1973, on possibly the most photographed cobblestone street in the West Country, and Thomas Hardy set some of his novels here, including part of *Jude the Obscure*, changing the town's name to 'Shaston'.

At the top of famous Gold Hill, and packed with historical information about the town, is the Gold Hill Museum and Garden. The museum brings to life the day-to-day events of Shaftesbury's inhabitants in years gone by. Exhibits include photos, artefacts, tools and original Dorset buttons. Away from the High Street, the museum's pretty cottage garden is a quiet place to sit and enjoy fantastic views of the hills and vales surrounding the town.

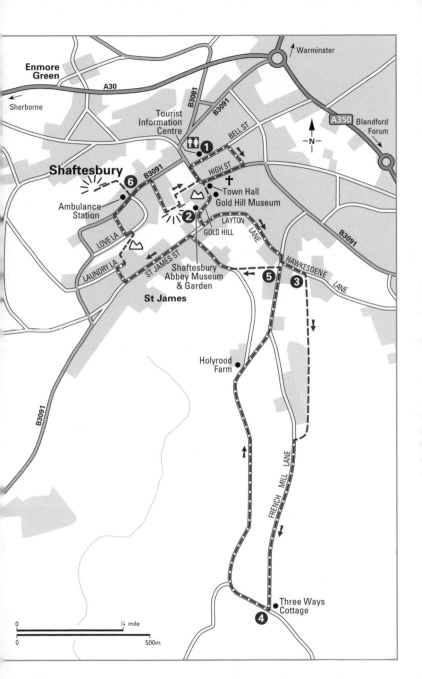

1. With your back to the window of the tourist information centre on Bell Street, turn left. Walk down to a terrace of houses. Turn right, down Mustons Lane. Pass a Palladian former church on the left, now a restaurant. At the High Street turn right. The High Street broadens into a market square by The Mitre pub, with medieval St Peter's Church and the town hall. Ahead is a line of shops and houses. Just after the town hall and before a postbox turn left down

a narrow lane; you'll suddenly find yourself at the top of picturesque Gold Hill, with a view of the green Dorset hills behind. At the top is the Town Museum.

2. The massive walls of Shaftesbury Abbey stand opposite the houses on Gold Hill. Walk down the hill to St James Street. Turn left into Layton Lane (no pavement) and follow the road along the contour of the hill. After 0.5 miles (800m), pass the junction with Shooters Lane on the left and, further on, the junction with French Mill Lane. Continue ahead up Hawkesdene Lane.

3. As you reach the top, turn right and go through a wooden kissing gate to enter Wilderness Park. Follow the grassy path above the trees and down. Go through a kissing gate at the end and turn immediately right, along the edge of the field. Cross a stile then turn left down the narrow lane. Continue for some 700yds (640m) until you reach Three Ways cottage, where you turn right.

4. Go forward along the lane, pass a turning to Gears Mill and follow the road as it climbs steadily back up to the town. After 0.5 miles (800m) pass Holyrood Farm on the left, and keep straight on up the hill, passing the junction with French Mill Lane on the right. Just after a postbox and before a crossroads, take the steep and uneven footpath down to the left.

5. Follow this leafy lane downhill and bear right at a junction, up a track which becomes Kingsman Lane. At the top turn left onto St James Street, packed with terraced cottages. Pass Ye Olde Two Brewers Inn on the left and pause to admire the Pump Yard, a pretty mews, further along on the right. Turn right, up Tanyard Lane. At the top turn right by some garages into Laundry Lane. Almost immediately turn left up Stoney Path, a steep and cobbled path (handrail). This leads to the top of town, and the views improve as you climb. At the top, take the left fork in the park and go through a small, iron kissing gate in the wall. Turn left along Love Lane and take the first path up to the right, called Langford Lane. At the end turn right. Cross the road and then, just beyond the ambulance station, turn left down a path between No. 37 and No. 35.

6. This leads to a vantage point with superb views to the north. Retrace your steps to the main road and turn left, passing Ox House. Cross over then turn right, down Abbey Walk, passing an old pump. Pass the curious Old School House on the left and turn left at the war memorial. Pass the entrance to the abbey ruins. At the end of the walkway keep left, to emerge at the High Street by the town hall and the top of Gold Hill. Turn left and then take the first turning on the right, into Bell Street, to return to the tourist information centre.

Where to eat and drink

Recommended in Shaftesbury are the Salt Cellar restaurant, Ye Olde Two Brewers Inn and Angola '76, a 'jungle café music bar'.

What to see

If you remember the 1970s then you will probably recognise Shaftesbury's Gold Hill. 'The Hovis advert' – a classic commercial – was shot here.

While you're there

The young King Edward the Martyr was reburied in Shaftesbury Abbey in AD 979, and it became a significant and very wealthy place of pilgrimage.

MARNHULL IN BLACKMOOR VALE

DISTANCE/TIME	4 miles (6.4km) / 2hrs
ASCENT/GRADIENT	90ft (27.5m) / ▲
PATHS	Village roads, farm tracks, footpaths
LANDSCAPE	Green vale, with distant views to low hills
SUGGESTED MAP	OS Explorer 129 Yeovil & Sherborne
START/FINISH	Grid reference: ST781192
DOG FRIENDLINESS	On lead on some sections of village roads. There are a lot of stiles
PARKING	Free car park at Marnhull village hall
PUBLIC TOILETS	None on route

In winter the fields of the broad Blackmoor Vale gleam and glint with standing water. The dampness and the soft, sweet air make for lush green meadows and, where there's rich pasture like this, there are dairy cattle. In Blackmoor Vale, there are thousands of mainly black and white Holstein-Friesians. In spring and summer they graze their way slowly through the fields on a regular routine. In late autumn, when the ground becomes too churned up, they are herded into byres, from where they stare out at passing walkers.

Any doubts that dairying is big business are soon dispelled in this part of Dorset, where a strong whiff of slurry often taints the wind. In recent years, dairy farming has faced some harsh economic realities, and some herds have been sold. One former dairy farm at Marnhull sold up and is now a maize producer – growing fodder for cattle elsewhere. Until the development of refrigeration and pasteurisation, milk was a highly perishable commodity. Dairy herds were kept on the fringes of towns to minimise the delay between milking and getting the milk to the consumer. Furthermore, prior to mechanisation, milking was a laborious, manual job and the risk of bacterial infection and contamination was much higher. Tess's experiences as a milkmaid in Thomas Hardy's novel *Tess of the D'Urbervilles* (1861) give a good picture of this way of rural life.

Everything changed with the advent of mass refrigeration, to slow the bacteria, and pasteurisation to kill them off. The cows are milked by vacuum suction pumps on the farm, and the efficiency is such that one cow can produce up to 1,320 gallons (6,000 litres) of milk in a year. Refrigerated road tankers transfer it to a central dairy where it is checked for bacteria before being pasteurised, processed and sent out, with an extended shop shelf-life. There are downsides to the success story, as with any industrial production or intensive farming, not least of which are concerns about livestock welfare. High levels of fertiliser and overflowing slurry pits contribute to around a quarter of water pollution incidents. Ruminating cattle produce vast amounts of methane gas, adding steadily to global warming. Yet it is estimated that we drink around four times as much of the white stuff as our predecessors.

17

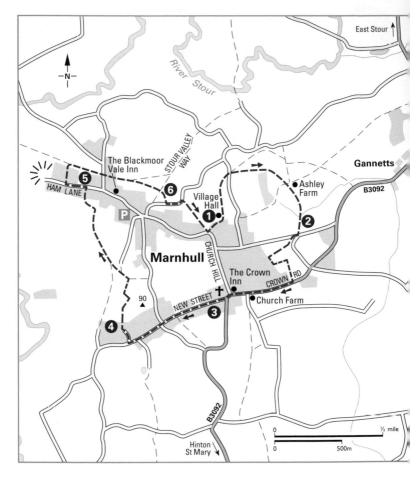

1. With the village hall on your right, and keeping the playground on your left, cross the recreation ground to two kissing gates in the far left corner. Go through and head right to another gate onto a lane. Turn left. Soon cross a stile buried in a hedge on your right and cross a field to a field gate and an overgrown stile in the hedge. Bear right across the field to a stile and walk past the Ashley Farm barn conversion and down the drive to the lane.

2. Turn right and look out for a stile on the left, just past a house and garden. Cross this and head diagonally right uphill to reach a gate. Do not go through but turn left here, cross a stile and head straight on to a fence. Turn left along the fence, then right – still following the fence – to cross two stiles and emerge onto Crown Road. Walk along, taking care to keep to the pavement (where one exists), until you reach the Crown Inn. Pass the pub and head towards the crossroads, with the church ahead.

3. Cross the road, keeping the church on your right, and follow residential New Street for approximately 0.75 miles (1.2km), taking the fourth right turning, with a fingerpost to Stour Valley Way, into Kentisworth Road.

4. At the road end bear right to go through a kissing gate, then follow the left fence to another kissing gate. Continue along the left edge of the field then, at the hedge end, head diagonally left and downhill to go through another kissing gate. Cross a plank bridge to head towards a new barn. Keep left of this and head through three gates in quick succession. In a few paces, pass some derelict farm buildings and take the gate to your left, then a field gate immediately afterwards. Walk along the ridge to go through two kissing gates. Walk along the top of the field then bear left between two bungalows into Ham Lane.

5. Turn left, past Dinhay, and take second right into Ham Meadows. Walk down here, ignoring a road on the left, and turn right and take the path between two bungalows, following this over a plank bridge and through a gate onto a grassy path. Go through the gate at the top and cross the road into Burges Close. Keep to the right to the end and take the path to the right between two houses, which leads to a stile. After the stile turn left, with a hedge on your right and open views to your left, and cross the next stile. Head right along the field edge to go through a kissing gate in the hedge into a narrow lane.

6. Turn left for about 200yds (180m), ignoring a waymark sign, and look out for steps up on the right leading over a low stile and into a field. Head diagonally right gently downhill towards the houses to reach the rear fence of the last house. Turn right by this, go through the field gate, turn left and take the first left (signposted Village Hall) to return to your car.

Where to eat and drink

Thomas Hardy immortalised both Marnhull pubs in *Tess of the D'Urbervilles* (he renamed the village Marlott). The smart-looking (and recently reopened) Blackmoor Vale Inn was his 'Rolliver's'. Today it serves home-made food and has a sizeable beer garden. Near the church is The Crown Inn (Hardy's 'Pure Drop'), with a priest hole, which leads to the church via a tunnel, as well as a low, thatched section from the 16th century. The Crown, too, serves food.

What to see

Marnhull's church is not always open, but, if you can get in, look for the memorial to John Warren, an 18th-century parish clerk and keen pipe smoker, who died at the ripe old age of 94. It is inscribed with a philosophical rhyme to John and his wife: 'And now there's no doubt, But their pipes are both out, Be it said without joke, That life is but smoke.'

While you're there

If you're hooked on Thomas Hardy's story, go to Bere Regis (his 'Kingsbere'). In the church are the canopied tombs of the Turberville family and a 15th-century window depicting the arms of the Turbervilles, all under an extraordinary carved and painted roof. The family died out but variations of their name lived on, which gave Hardy the starting point for his novel.

FONTMELL DOWN AND MELBURY HILL

DISTANCE/TIME	4.5 miles (7.2km) / 2hrs
ASCENT/GRADIENT	820ft (250m) / ▲ ▲
PATHS	Downland tracks, muddy bridleway, village lanes
LANDSCAPE	Rolling downland with superb views
SUGGESTED MAP	OS Explorer 118 Shaftesbury & Cranborne Chase
START/FINISH	Grid reference: ST886187
DOG FRIENDLINESS	Some road walking
PARKING	Car park on road south of Shaftesbury, with National Trust sign for Fontmell Down in the bottom left corner
PUBLIC TOILETS	None on route

Since the end of World War II over 80 per cent of the chalk downs in England have been altered or lost because enriching artificial fertilisers have been introduced and land has been claimed for arable crops. Grazing is the key, in a scheme first introduced by the Neolithic farmers. Without grazing, the close-cropped grass of the downs would soon revert to scrub and woodland. Modern management is therefore based on restoring the old farming cycles of grazing by sheep and cattle and maintaining the land for the benefit of threatened wildlife as well as for agricultural output. Preservation of the precious habitat of the outstanding area of Melbury and Fontmell Downs is in the hands of the National Trust, with assistance from the Dorset Wildlife Trust.

A chief beneficiary of this policy is the butterfly, for more than 35 species have been recorded here. Some have very specific requirements for their survival. The silver-spotted skipper, for example, breeds in only 14 places in Britain, and only one in Dorset – Fontmell Down. It lays its eggs on the underside of sheep's fescue grass, but the grass has to be just the right length. If the juicy new grass shoots are nibbled by the sheep in August, the caterpillars will starve. Adonis blues are hardly less demanding – they need a tightly packed, south-facing, warm, grassy slope. The grand-sounding Duke of Burgundy fritillary, on the other hand, likes to live on the edge of the sward, that is, where the cowslips blossom in springtime.

The wealth and variety of wild flowers found on these chalky downs is the other delight. They thrive on the poorer soils, not squeezed out by faster-growing monocultures. In summer look for the vivid violet-blue specks of early gentians in the turf, the tiny stalked spikes of the mauve milkwort and the deeper purple of thyme. They give way in autumn to the browny yellow flowers of the carline thistle and the spiralling, white-flowered spikes of autumn lady's tresses. In autumn, this is a place to find glow-worms. About the length of a fingernail, these little creatures were once a common sight. It is the females who glow. Wingless and defenceless, they hide during the day, but at night crawl onto vegetation to shine their lower abdomens upwards to attract males.

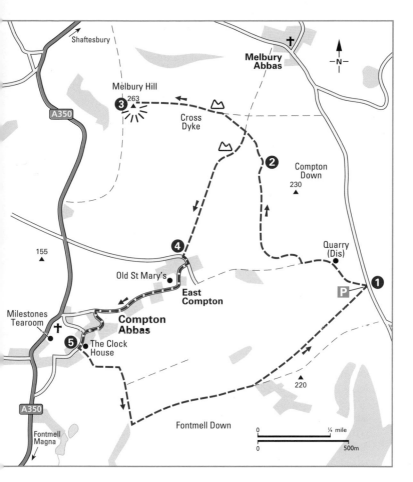

1. Take the rough track from the bottom right corner of the car park, walking downhill towards Compton Abbas. Pass an old chalk quarry. Soon turn right up some wooden steps and cross a stile to access Compton Down. Bear left and uphill towards a fence, and eventually join it at a corner. Pick up a narrow cattle path just below the fence to contour down and around the shoulder of the Down, heading towards the saddle between the Down and Melbury Hill.

2. Pass a steep, natural amphitheatre on your left and continue dropping gently to join the saddle at a fingerpost and gate. Turn left here to head upwards to the top of Melbury Hill – a steep climb but well worth it for the views. Pass the scar of an ancient cross dyke, on the left as you climb, and look down the other side to the silvery tower of Melbury Abbas church.

3. A toposcope marks the top of the hill, with fantastic views all around, including Shaftesbury on its ridge to the north and the ridges of Hambledon Hill to the southeast. Retrace your route to the signpost and gate. Ignore the signposted bridleway and turn half right across the grass to join a track coming in from the left. Shortly, at the end of the field below you, bear down steeply left to three gates and go through two of them. Head straight along

the field-edge towards Compton Abbas. Pass through a gate to emerge onto a road.

4. Turn left and follow this road right round a sharp bend. Pass the tower of the original church, isolated in its small graveyard. Continue along the lane, passing houses of varying ages. Descend between high hedges and turn left at the junction. Continue on this winding road through the bottom of the village, passing attractive, stone-built, thatched cottages.

5. Pass the Clock House and turn left up the bridleway, signposted 'Gore Clump'. The gravel track – which often doubles as a stream – gives way to a tree-lined path between the fields. Go through a gate and continue straight on. Go up the right edge of this and the next field. In the corner, turn left along a fence and walk up the track above some trees to reach a gate and National Trust sign for Fontmell Down. Pass through this onto Fontmell Down. Continue straight ahead on the rising track. After 0.5 miles (800m) ignore the gate to the right and keep straight ahead along the fence, to reach the top of the hill and the car park.

Where to eat and drink

Compton Abbas boasts the 17th-century Milestones Tearoom, just south of the church and accessible from the main road. It promises morning coffee, lunches and afternoon teas, and if the weather is sunny you can take your refreshments in the patio garden.

What to see

As you walk towards Compton Abbas, pause at the churchyard of old St Mary's. Rest a moment on the great mounting block by the wall, to admire the ancient farmhouse opposite. All that remains of the old church is the ghostly, pale tower, blocked up and left to the pigeons. In the graveyard itself are some crumbling tombs and the weathered stump of an old cross. A new St Mary's was built within the village in 1866.

While you're there

Just east of here, over the border in Wiltshire, Win Green Hill (another National Trust property) is crowned by a ring of trees. It's the highest point of the ancient royal forest of Cranborne Chase, and the views are superb. When he tired of the hunt, King John hung out at nearby Tollard Royal.

THE ROYAL FOREST OF CRANBORNE CHASE

DISTANCE/TIME	4 miles (6.4km) / 2hrs
ASCENT/GRADIENT	165ft (50m) / ▲ ▲
PATHS	Woodland paths and tracks, quiet roads, farm paths
LANDSCAPE	Woods and valleys of Cranborne Chase
SUGGESTED MAP	OS Explorer 118 Shaftesbury & Cranborne Chase
START/FINISH	Grid reference: SU003194
DOG FRIENDLINESS	Strict control required in RSPB woods
PARKING	Garston Wood car park (free), on Bowerchalke road
PUBLIC TOILETS	None on route

Cranborne Chase covers around 100sq miles (260sq km) of the long chalk massif that straddles the Dorset/Wiltshire border east of Shaftesbury. Once a royal hunting preserve, it is now rolling grassland with pockets of mixed woodland. Compared with other parts of Dorset, there are few settlements here, a sign of the feudal state in which the land was held until 1830. Like most of southern England after the last ice age, Dorset became smothered in a natural growth of native, broadleaved woodland, such as oak, ash and elm. As the human population spread, this woodland was gradually cleared, firstly for its valuable timber and secondly to make way for agricultural land. The hunting 'forest' of Cranborne Chase claimed by William the Conqueror included open sections of heath, downland, scrub and rough pasture, as well as patches of remaining woodland. Little original forest remains on the Chase – most woods show signs of mixed planting and many generations of coppicing.

The effects of planting for timber in the late 18th century can be seen in the widespread stands of non-native beech across the Chase. Trees for timber were planted compactly to encourage tall, straight growth. Coppicing, the chief form of woodland management, was designed to produce a continuous supply of timber for everyday use. Hazel that was cut back or coppiced when young would grow long, straight poles. Repeating the exercise produced a steady supply of timber for thatching spars, hurdles and other uses. The resulting multi-stemmed growths, or stools, can be seen today all over Dorset's woods and include oak, ash, alder, sweet chestnut and even sycamore. In Garston Wood you can see the effects of modern coppicing in action on hazel and field maple. The seven- to eight-year cycle of cutting means that there are different stages of tree development within the one wood, creating more light and space than if it were left unmanaged. This produces an optimum habitat for wildlife, including sunlight-loving butterflies such as the silver-washed fritillary and purple hairstreak.

The pursuit of fallow deer on the Chase provided the mainstay of royal sport. The deer can still be seen here. Cranborne Chase changed hands many times, and the hunting rights were acquired by King John and retained by most succeeding monarchs until the 17th century. In 1714 they passed to the Pitt-Rivers family, who ruled the area like feudal overlords. Operating under so-called Chase Law and free from normal policing, Cranborne became a byway for smugglers and a refuge for criminals, often with bloody results – especially when conflicts arose over poaching. In 1830, after considerable local pressure, Chase Law was abandoned and life became a little more settled.

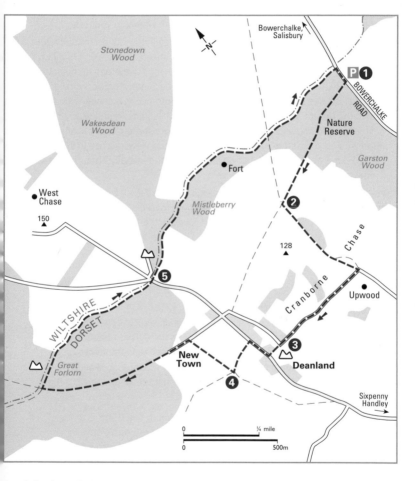

1. Go through the gate in the corner and take the broad track that leads up through the woods. Go straight ahead through a kissing gate and emerge at the corner of a field. Keep right for a few paces up the edge of this field to the first corner, then head straight across the field.

2. At the hedge corner, turn left following the waymark sign and walk along the bridleway with the hedge to your left, through rolling farmland dotted with trees. The muddy farm track leads gently downhill. Where it sweeps left into the farm, go straight ahead on a grassy track. Pass some cow byres on the left,

with Upwood farmhouse largely hidden in some trees ahead, and turn right along the lane. Continue through a gate, along an old avenue of sycamores between high banks and hedges.

3. Pass a house hedge on the right and, where the track sweeps right to a lane, bear left on a steep, narrow path straight down the hill to emerge on a road, in the hamlet of Deanland. Turn right, pass a phone box that now serves as a local information booth and reach a footpath on the left with a yellow marker. Bear diagonally right through a copse to go through a gap with the remains of a stile, then bear left up the edge of the field, with woods to your left.

4. Don't miss a stile on your left, and turn right by it, to walk across the field, parallel with the road. Over the brow of the hill ahead, the pleasing higgledy-piggledy settlement of New Town can be seen. Head for the gap in the bottom corner of the field. Turn left up the lane, which becomes a broad, woodland track. Follow this for 0.5 miles (800m). By the entrance to a conifer wood, named the Great Forlorn, look for the 'Sixpenny Handley Roundwalk' waymarker and turn right up the hill. After a short sharp climb it levels out, with fields on your left. Keep straight on, with good views across to West Chase House, at the head of its own valley. Descend steadily, then cross a stile to emerge at a road by a lodge house.

5. Cross straight over onto a broad track and immediately turn up to the right on a narrow path by an electricity pole and waymarker. Follow this straight up the hill through the woods – it levels out towards the top, with fields on the left. Ignore a path leading to the left. At a T-junction of tracks, in front of a large wooden gate, turn left then bear right, along the edge of the wood, eventually descending to reach the road. Turn right to return to the car park.

Where to eat and drink

The Roebuck Inn free house at Sixpenny Handley serves real ale and traditional, home-cooked food in its bright and airy front restaurant. Try vegetarian lasagne, cod and chips, baguettes, jacket potatoes or something else from the wide range. A Sunday roast lunch is served throughout winter. In summer there's a beer garden; dogs are welcome.

What to see

Listen for the nightingale's song in Garston Wood. The RSPB is trying to balance its needs against those of the endangered turtle dove in its management of the wood. In the early 1980s a young commercial plantation of beech, larch and Corsican pine drew the nightingales. By 1993 the dense understorey in which they thrived had been smothered by the tree canopy, and they disappeared. The plantation is gradually being felled and replanted to provide a suitable habitat for the nightingales.

While you're there

Sixpenny Handley has one of the oddest names in England. The prefix derives from a mix of English and Celtic words and means 'hill of the Saxons'. Much of the old village was destroyed in a fire in 1892. Today it's a lively and modern village.

PENTRIDGE DOWN AND BOKERLEY DYKE

DISTANCE/TIME	3.5 miles (5.7km) / 2hrs
ASCENT/GRADIENT	475ft (145m) / ▲ ▲ ▲
PATHS	Steep, muddy farmland, grassy sward, farm roads
LANDSCAPE	Chalk downs, open grassland, fields and copse
SUGGESTED MAP	OS Explorer 118 Shaftesbury & Cranborne Chase
START/FINISH	Grid reference: SU034178
DOG FRIENDLINESS	No problems but control needed past farms and dogs must be on leads through nature reserve
PARKING	Lay-by in Pentridge or start from car park at Martin Down NNR
PUBLIC TOILETS	None on route

At 607ft (185m) high, Penbury Knoll has made a good lookout over Cranborne Chase since settlers first left their mark on this quiet corner of northeast Dorset some 5,000 years ago. The maps show signs of Celtic field systems (associated with the period around 1000 BC) plotted around the lovely green combe of Pentridge Down, though little is revealed to the naked eye. The extraordinary Dorset Cursus (processional way) starts to the north of here, and the landscape is littered with lumpy burial mounds, or tumuli, and long barrows. Grim's Ditch marked a Bronze Age farm boundary, but a more significant defensive earthwork remains from this period, constructed to protect the long-vanished hill-fort.

Bokerley Dyke (Bokerley Ditch on the OS map) consists of a high bank and deep ditch, which originally extended for some 3 miles (4.8km). A matter of weeks' work for a JCB, the construction of the dyke must have taken thousands of hours of punishing hard labour. In the fourth century AD it was strengthened and parts of it were re-dug, as by then it formed an important defence against Saxon invaders on the Roman route along Ackling Dyke to the stronghold at Badbury Rings. In the 9th century it again formed a vital part of Dorset's defences – this time from attacks by the Vikings, who were overrunning the Kingdom of Wessex. King Ethelred I was mortally wounded in a fierce battle on Martin Down, on the other side of the dyke, in AD 871. This event opened the way for his younger brother, Alfred, to claim the throne of Wessex and eventually make peace with the marauding Danes.

There has been a settlement below the hill at Pentridge since at least the Domesday survey in the 11th century, when St Rumbold's Church received its first mention. The quiet hamlet of Pentridge is spared the modern invasion of traffic passing through. Tiled cob walls mix with flint and brick and thatch, and there's a handsome 18th-century barn. Unusually, little Chestnut Cottage, by the turning to the church, has exposed timbers. Unlike busier villages, houses here are set back from the single main street, tucked behind hedges and gardens, or in a silent line up the hill. There's no street lighting. In the dusk, little squares of golden light appear, unshaded by curtains, evoking memories of Thomas Hardy's obsession in *The Woodlanders* (1887) with lamps and firelight and looking through people's windows to see life played out.

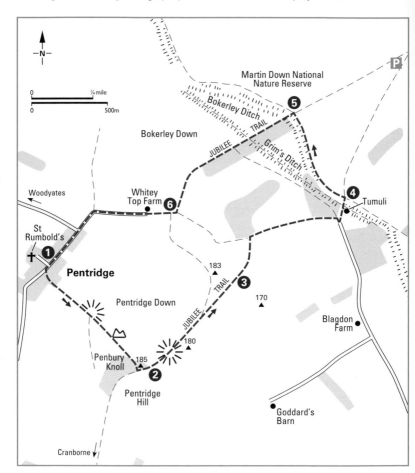

1. From the lay-by walk past the turning up to the church and cross the stile on the left by the footpath sign. Head up the field to a stile, and cross it to enter a narrow footpath. This leads between hedges up towards the 607ft (185m) Pentridge Hill. Cross another stile into a field and keep straight ahead. As you pause to catch your breath, you can start to admire the view opening around you, with the green curve of Pentridge Down on the left. Keep straight on to the top of the hill (Penbury Knoll), following a tractor track and then peeling off to the right on a vague path to aim for a stile in front of some trees. Head for the left side of this little spinney.

2. Pass the trig point and continue forward a few paces to a track. Turn left onto the Jubilee Trail footpath, which runs along the ridge of the down beside

an ancient hedge line. (There are fabulous views on either side – Pentridge is largely hidden in the trees.) Keep right at two forks to continue along the fence line. After 0.5 miles (800m) the path starts to descend.

3. Go through a gate into a copse, following the Jubilee Trail marker. Soon bear diagonally left across a field to a fingerpost on the opposite side beside the trees and turn right down the side of the field. There are good views of Bokerley Dyke curving away to your left. Look for a gap in the thick hedge to your left and descend through woodland, bearing immediately right to a gate. Go through and turn right, on to a bridleway. Pass a metal gate and immediately hook back left on a chalky track. As you start to descend, curious mounds appear to the right – these are tumuli.

4. Cross Grim's Ditch and Bokerley Dyke onto Martin Down National Nature Reserve. Look for the information board on your left. Immediately turn left onto the grassy path, with the ditch on your left (the main track continues down to the Martin Down NNR car park). Follow this downhill for 0.5 miles (800m).

5. At a cross track junction at the bottom of the dip, turn left along the Jubilee Trail, passing a fingerpost which announces that it's only 90 miles (144km) to Forde Abbey (the bridleway to the right heads to Martin Down NNR car park). A nettley path runs up the side of mixed woodland before joining a track. At the end of the woods go straight ahead, through a gate. Follow the field boundary on your right up to a stile at the top.

6. Just before the stile, turn right down the bridleway for 55yds (50m) and go through two gates onto an enclosed track. Pentridge Down emerges to the left, with the village hidden by trees. Pass through another gate onto a farm track between high hedges at Whitey Top Farm. Continue down to the bottom and follow it round to the left. Walk back into the village along the main street to return to your car.

Where to eat and drink

There's nothing in the immediate vicinity of Pentridge, but that's a good excuse to visit the attractive red-brick village of Cranborne, to the southeast. Top of the list for real ale is the Sheaf of Arrows pub in the square. Savour your pint in the terrace garden beside the pub. Further choice is offered at the popular garden-centre tea rooms by Cranborne Manor (the Manor gardens are open on Wednesdays in summer).

What to see

St Rumbold's Church was rebuilt in 1855 and is a pleasing, unfussy structure of grey stone and flint. Look for a plaque inside commemorating one Robert Browning who died in 1746: he was a butler and the great-great-grandfather of the famous Victorian poet of the same name.

While you're there

Explore Martin Down, on the other side of the Dyke, and just over the border into Hampshire. A National Nature Reserve in the care of Natural England, it consists of open tracts of chalk downland, dotted with wild flowers including purple clover, lilac-coloured scabious and soft blue harebells, with heath, scrub and woodland.

THROUGH ASHMORE WOOD

DISTANCE/TIME	5.75 miles (9.2km) / 2hrs 30min
ASCENT/GRADIENT	427ft (130m) / ▲
PATHS	Forestry and farm tracks, woodland and field paths
LANDSCAPE	Mixed woodland, quiet village
SUGGESTED MAP	OS Explorer 118 Shaftesbury & Cranborne Chase
START/FINISH	Grid reference: ST897167
DOG FRIENDLINESS	One short stretch of road walking
PARKING	At Washers Pit entrance to Ashmore Wood
PUBLIC TOILETS	None on route

To anyone familiar with the monotonous, sterile conifer forests of northern Britain, the plantations of Dorset are a revelation and a delight. Best among these are the Forestry Commission's woods around Ashmore. At the time of the Domesday Book around 15 per cent of the land area of England was covered by woodland. A survey undertaken in 2000 put that figure at 8.4 per cent, with oak accounting for a quarter of all broadleaved trees.

The Forestry Commission was set up as a government body in 1919, partly in response to the timber shortage created by the needs of booming industry in the 18th and 19th centuries. Furthermore, timber shortage had been identified as a critical problem during World War I. Not only was timber required for making pit props for coal mines, but trench warfare also swallowed up vast quantities for shoring up and lining the trenches. The Commission's early brief – to grow as much timber as possible in as short a time as possible – has changed over the years. Nowadays, sensitivity to local soil conditions, conservation and the needs of wildlife, and public access for leisure also play a part in the choice of how a woodland is managed.

As you walk down Ashmore Wood's broad tracks you'll notice an appealing variety of smaller tree species planted along the margins, and plenty of bird nesting boxes. Although obviously plantation woodland, it represents replanting on the site of much older woods. Ashmore is therefore rich in wild flowers, especially bluebells in late spring, but also celandines, primroses and the tall spears of great mullein and foxgloves. The forestry planting is a combination of broadleaved woodland and mixed conifers. The beech trees, magnificent in their autumn colour, stifle most things growing in the shade at the base of their trunks, but harbour the best sites for fungi. Beneath the conifers emerald moss grows in pillowy mounds.

Ashmore village is the highest in Dorset and stands on the border with Wiltshire. The village is on the road to nowhere in particular and has no pub, so has remained pleasantly uncommercial and feels like a discovery. Thatched houses cluster around a large circular duck pond. The greenish tinge that gives an old-fashioned air to its houses comes from the colour of the local sandstone. Spare a glance for the corbelled end wall of Manor Farm, which may have been lifted from Eastbury House.

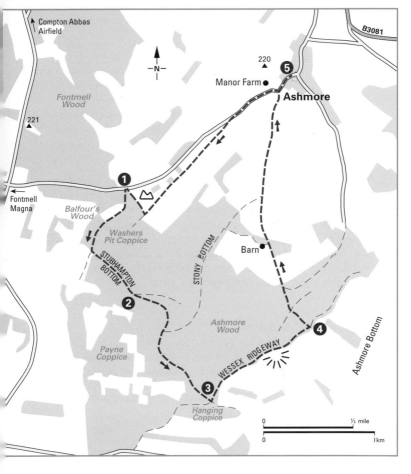

1. With your back to the road, walk past the barrier and follow the firm forestry road as it curves past the beeches of Washers Pit Coppice on your left and Balfour's Wood on your right. After 0.5 miles (800m) ignore a bridleway up to the right and keep going straight ahead on the track. You're now in Stubhampton Bottom, following a quiet winding valley through the trees.

2. Where the main track swings up to the left, keep straight ahead, following the blue public bridleway marker, on a rutted track along the valley floor. A path from Stony Bottom feeds in from the left – keep straight on. Where there's an area of smaller coppiced trees on the hillside on your left, ignore a path peeling off to the right and shortly afterwards follow the blue bridleway markers onto a narrow track to the right which runs down through coppiced woodland parallel and below the forestry road. At Hanging Coppice a marker

post shows where the Wessex Ridgeway path feeds in from the right – again, keep straight ahead. The path soon rises to emerge in trees at the corner of a field.

3. Turn left at the fence (follow the blue marker) to walk uphill. Follow this path along the edge of the forest carpeted with bluebells in spring and with glimpses of lovely views to the southeast.

4. After 0.75 miles (1.2km) turn left at a junction of tracks (signposted 'Ashmore') and walk through the woods. Cross over a track and keep straight on, following the blue marker, to meet a track. Go straight on, following signs for Ashmore, and soon emerging from the forest; ignore two left turns. Continue straight up this track for about 1 mile (1.6km), through farmland and across the exposed open hilltop, with the houses of Ashmore village coming into view. At the end of the track turn right and walk into the village to the pond.

5. From the village retrace your route, remaining on the road beyond the point where the track joined it. Pass Manor Farm on the right and head gently downhill. Just before the road narrows to single-track width, bear left through a gate (blue marker). Walk along the top of the field, pass a gate on the left and bear slightly down to the right to go through the lower of two gates at the far side. Walk straight ahead on a broad green track. Go through a gate into the woods and immediately turn right, following a steep bridleway straight down the side of the hill to emerge by the car park.

Where to eat and drink
Compton Abbas Airfield has a café and bar, serving good home cooking. It's open throughout the year. On offer are an all-day breakfast, morning coffee, lunches, baguettes and bar snacks, afternoon tea and so on. While the setting may not be highly sophisticated, the views are fantastic. You could even book a trial flight while you're there.

What to see
Opposite the pond in Ashmore, the war memorial cross records the names of local members of the Dorset Regiment and Dorset Yeomanry who died in World War I. There is just one addition to the roll for World War II: G Coombs, a pilot with the South African Air Force (SAAF), who died in 1942.

While you're there
Drive down into the pretty village of Fontmell Magna, along an attractive route that brings you in past a big duck pond. A sign on your left by a little bridge marks the shallow sheep wash in the stream. This was used for washing sheep until modern dips were introduced in the 1930s. The houses just beyond The Fontmell pub, noted for its food, once housed the Fontmell Potteries, recalling the days when this was a centre of terracotta making.

MARNHULL AND HINTON ST MARY

DISTANCE/TIME	5 miles (8km) / 4hrs
ASCENT/GRADIENT	300ft (91m) / ▲
PATHS	Field paths and tracks, some lanes
LANDSCAPE	Rolling farmland
SUGGESTED MAP	OS Explorer 129 Yeovil & Sherborne
START/FINISH	Grid reference: ST786160
DOG FRIENDLINESS	Beware of electric fences in fields; control needed through farmyards and care across high bridges
PARKING	On Ridgeway Lane by St Mary's church
PUBLIC TOILETS	None en route

With church, pub and manor house surrounded by a charming miscellany of gardened cottages, some dating back to the 16th century, Hinton St Mary is just one of Dorset's many attractive villages. But it became set apart in 1963, when the village blacksmith uncovered fragments of an extensive Roman mosaic. Excavation revealed an almost complete floor, extending across two rooms and combining classical hunting and pagan scenes with a central roundel portraying the bust of a man before a Chi-Rho symbol. Interpreted as the image of Christ, it is one of the earliest known representations and the only such floor mosaic. The rooms are thought to have been part of a villa, possibly a dining or reception room or perhaps the private chapel of the villa's owner. The mosaic is now in the British Museum.

Before the Dissolution of the Monasteries, the village was a lay-settlement and small nunnery of St Mary's Abbey Church at Shaftsbury. The estate was eventually bought by Sir William Pitt, who held high office successively under Elizabeth I, James I and Charles I, and has passed through various branches of the family to the present day. One of the most notable family members was Augustus Pitt Rivers, who, after a career in the army, inherited the Cranborne estates. Already a passionate collector of ethnographic artefacts, he began a methodical excavation of local prehistoric sites, recording the finds and their context. He was appointed the first Inspector of Ancient Monuments and is regarded as a founder of modern archaeology.

More scattered, Marnhull lies to the north on a limestone prominence that provided stone for many of the buildings. Village history begins with Saxon charters of the 10th century, but archaeological excavation in the locality has discovered Iron Age and Roman settlements together with a cemetery containing over 20 Romano-British skeletons. Nash Court, just to the north, originally belonged to Glastonbury Abbey, but Henry VIII bestowed it upon Catherine Parr, his final wife. Overlooking Blackmore Vale, the area was traditionally given to dairy farming, and in Thomas Hardy's *Tess of the*

D'Urbervilles, Marnhull became 'Marlott', the birthplace of his ill-fated heroine, who buried her baby in the churchyard of St Peter's. The tale wanders across the Wessex countryside before reaching its tragic climax at Stonehenge.

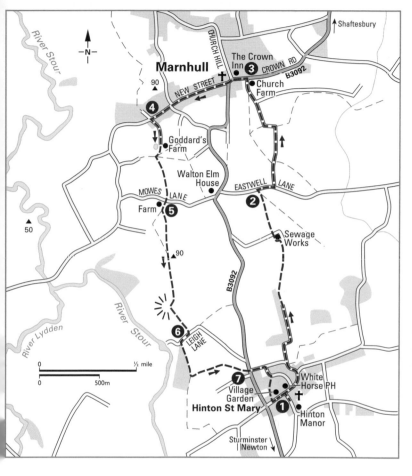

1. Walk up from the church and turn right in front of the White Horse. Pass a side street then shortly fork left by Barley Yard House. Reaching a sharp bend, leave through a waymarked gate on the right. Turn left and follow a track downhill towards a wood. Wind right and left to carry on along a rough track within a belt of trees. Bearing slightly right, continue across a field to a plank bridge. Maintain the heading across another field to an indented corner and bear left beside trees screening a small sewage plant. Cross a track to a stiled bridge and head up by the right hedge to Eastwell Lane.

2. Go right to a bend by a cottage and turn off left along a farm track. At a junction, swing left and then right, later keeping ahead past stock sheds at Church Farm to emerge at Marnhull.

3. Head left past The Crown Inn and keep straight on at a junction along New Street.

4. After 0.5 mile (800m), opposite Kentisworth Road, turn left along a lane. At Goddard's Farm, bear right to skirt a pond and walk up beside the left hedge to a gap. Wind through consecutive gates and follow the right hedge, slipping over a stile at its end and continuing beyond the end of the left fence to a gate in the corner. Keep going by the right hedge to come out at Mowes Lane.

5. Joining a path beside the gate opposite, bypass a farmyard to the field behind. Head away by the left boundary to a gate and stile in the corner. The ongoing path leads past a wooded pool to continue at the left edge of another field. Through consecutive gates at the bottom corner, go right at the top of the next field. Pass through a gap and swing left above a final field to cross a stile and emerge onto Leigh Lane.

6. Walk downhill for 150yds (137m) then leave left on a bridleway signed to Wood Lane. Wind left and right to follow a grass track through a plantation. Where the track swings left, continue forward to emerge at the edge of a field. Go left up the edge, swinging within the top corner. Reaching a stile, cross it and then another and bear right along the hedge in the adjacent field. Turn within the corner to a gate, exiting onto a track between hedges that leads out left to a lane at the edge of Hinton St Mary.

7. Take the lane opposite and go first right. On the bend, leave ahead through a metal field gate and cross a small field to a gap in the hedge/fence behind houses. Walk out to a street that returns you to the junction beside the White Horse.

Where to eat and drink

Thomas Hardy re-brands The Crown Inn at Marnhull as the 'Pure Drop Inn', and in his novel it is where Tess's father celebrates the discovery of his noble descent. Full of charm, with an inglenook fireplace, oak beams and a priest hole, it offers visitors a selection of fine ales and refreshments. Food is served all day from noon to 9pm (9.30pm at weekends) at the bar, outside in the beer garden or in the restaurant. Back at Hinton, there's the welcoming White Horse, which has a great reputation for both its food and beer. The pub is dog friendly and there is a comfortable garden for when the weather is fine.

What to see

Look out for the Village Garden in Hinton by the White Horse, where there is an information panel describing the Roman mosaic. The garden was established to celebrate the Millennium.

While you're there

There's a small museum in nearby and pretty Sturminster Newton, which highlights its past as a cattle market and dairy town. Thomas Hardy lived there for a while after his marriage to Emma, and described it as one of the happiest times in his life. It was at Sturminster that he wrote *The Return of the Native*.

PURSE CAUNDLE CIRCUIT

DISTANCE/TIME	5 miles (8km) / 2hrs
ASCENT/GRADIENT	427ft (130m) / ▲
PATHS	Muddy field paths, farm tracks, country roads, wet bridleway (wellies recommended)
LANDSCAPE	Little green hills and valleys with scattered settlements
SUGGESTED MAP	OS Explorer 129 Yeovil & Sherborne
START/FINISH	Grid reference: ST695175
DOG FRIENDLINESS	Some road walking
PARKING	Limited space by church, Purse Caundle
PUBLIC TOILETS	None on route

On the north Dorset border, Purse Caundle is too easily bypassed by folk in a hurry to reach Sherborne. It is an ordinary little village with an extraordinarily fine manor house. On the village lane you are almost too close to admire it properly – you get a better overall view of its extent from the hillside opposite, towards the end of this walk.

The present manor dates from the early 15th century. It is said to be haunted by various spirits of its rich past. For example, on Midsummer Eve you may hear the howling of a pack of hounds, no doubt on the scent of a ghostly stag. In the 13th century the lodge house here was a haven where royal hunting dogs, wounded in the chase in the deer forests of Blackmoor, could be brought for rest and recovery under the care of the steward, John Godwyne.

For this important service Godwyne was granted the manor of Purse Caundle. Such whimsical royal patronage was not untypical in Dorset. On a similar basis, the manor of Winfrith was granted to the man who held the King's washbasin on His Royal Highness's birthday, and that of Kingston Russell to a widow who was responsible for putting the King's chess pieces back in the box when His Majesty had finished playing. The manor, minus the dogs, was eventually sold on for the handsome price of 100 silver marks to a Richard Long, who started building the present structure around 1429. Another ghost apparently lived in an old well and made his presence known by chasing ladies upstairs. When that got too much, the well was filled in and the staircase dismantled. Robbed of his fun, the ghost was seen no more.

From the outside, in daylight, the manor house looks mellow enough, guarded by a stone boar on the driveway. The slim oriel window overlooking the road conceals the Great Chamber, and there's a splendid beamed roof in the Great Hall. It has changed hands many times through the centuries, most notably during the Civil War, when William Hanham, whose carved initials proclaim him responsible for much of the later building of the house, picked the losing side and lost everything to the Commonwealth. The manor is still privately owned but is occasionally opened to the public – see it if you can.

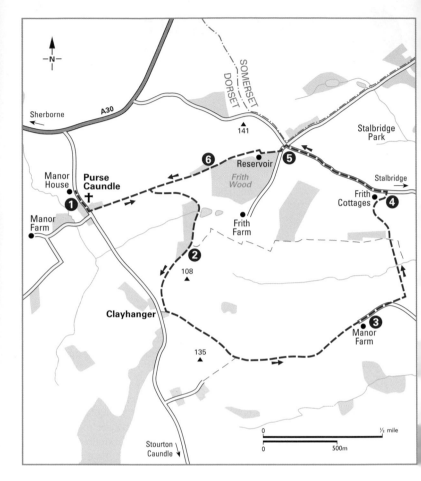

1. Park by the church, where there is a memorial bench in honour of four local men who were killed in World War I. Walk up the village street to admire the manor house. Return, pass the phone box and postbox, and turn left through a field gate. Go straight up the edge of the field, cross a stile and turn right to continue on this line, up through a gateway and across another field. After a second gateway bear diagonally right up the field. Cross a stile in the far corner and turn right. Soon take a hedge gap on your right and pass a lake to your left. Take a hole through the hedge and bear right along the next field-edge.

2. Go through a gate then over a narrow stile at the corner and go on down the field edge on the right, until you go through a gate on the right by the houses of Clayhanger. Before reaching the road, turn left, up a bridleway. This narrows and is shared with a stream. It's also apt to become extremely overgrown in the summer. Go through a gate and head diagonally out across the field, slanting up to find a faint track. Go through the field gate in the far, top corner onto the muddy track. This becomes a hedged lane, which you follow for 0.5 miles (800m) to pass Manor Farm.

3. In 120yds (110m), go over a stile and bear right to pass through a field gate and head forward to a stile next to a gateway. Go straight down the field to cross a footbridge in the middle of the hedge. Keep the same line down the next field, to a gate and a footbridge. Turn left to follow the left field-edge uphill and bear right in front of a pair of dwellings called Frith Cottages onto a road.

4. Turn left on the road and walk up it for 0.5 miles (800m), beside the stone wall of Stalbridge Park, to a crossroads.

5. Turn left, towards Frith Farm. In 50yds (45m) bear right, following markers. The track bends left, through a gate to a covered reservoir. Pass to the right of this and turn right, through a gate. Descend some steps and turn left down the edge of the field. Continue straight on through a gap, now with views to the manor.

6. At the bottom keep forward into woodland. Walk down this, then scramble around trees to cross the ditch on the left and turn right down the edge of the field. Go through a gateway and retrace your route to the church.

Where to eat and drink
Purse Caundle has a larger neighbour to the south, Stourton Caundle, with picturesque stone houses, a little schoolhouse with a belfry, and a grey stone church tucked to one side. The village pub is a free house called The Trooper, particularly recommended for its beer.

What to see
The massive encircling wall of Stalbridge Park, silvered with lichen, creates an eager expectation of a glimpse of a great house. It's an anticipation fed by the massive gateway beside the road to the north of Stalbridge. You'll peer in vain, however, for the mansion was demolished in 1822 and never replaced.

While you're there
Drop into Stalbridge for a couple of pleasant-looking pubs – The Stalbridge Arms (which has its own skittle alley) and The Swan – and to admire the 15th-century village cross, which holds up the traffic on the long, narrow high street. Tall, slim and golden, its features are well worn by time. The cross head is a modern replica – the original fell off in the 1950s.

SIR WALTER RALEIGH'S SHERBORNE

DISTANCE/TIME	6.5 miles (10.4km) / 3hrs
ASCENT/GRADIENT	443ft (135m) / ▲ ▲
PATHS	Country lanes, green lane, field paths, estate tracks
LANDSCAPE	Gentle hills and dairy villages south of Sherborne, open parkland, woodland
SUGGESTED MAP	OS Explorer 129 Yeovil & Sherborne
START/FINISH	Grid reference: ST670157
DOG FRIENDLINESS	Some road walking; on leads in the Deer Park
PARKING	On road by church, Haydon village, 2 miles (3.2km) southeast of Sherborne
PUBLIC TOILETS	None on route

Sir Walter Raleigh was an adventurer-cum-privateer, navigator, courtier and poet. His lasting legacies are the staples of tobacco and potatoes. A Devon man, born in 1552, he came to the attention of Queen Elizabeth I. Consequently he sailed off to the Americas to claim new lands for her and to plunder Spanish treasure ships along the way. By the time he returned, in 1587, his light at court was being outshone by the youthful 2nd Earl of Essex.

Raleigh, then around 40, fell madly in love with the much younger Elizabeth Throckmorton, the Queen's maid of honour. She became pregnant and they married in secret. When the Queen found out, she was furious and imprisoned them both in the Tower of London briefly, before banishing them from her sight. Raleigh had earlier acquired the Norman castle at Sherborne, formerly owned by the Bishop of Salisbury. He moved there with Elizabeth and their child, but the old castle proved inadequate. In 1594 he built a new, fashionably square house with corner towers on the opposite riverbank. He constructed water gardens and a bowling green, planted exotic trees brought back from his travels and entertained London friends. It is said he loved Sherborne 'above all his possessions, of all places on earth'. But he went to sea again, this time to explore the coast of Trinidad and the Orinoco River, joining in the Sack of Cadiz in 1596. His role as Governor of Jersey in the Channel Islands also took him away from home in 1600. In 1603, perceived as a threat to the new monarch after the death of Elizabeth, Raleigh was sentenced to death. This was commuted to life imprisonment and, after 13 years in the Tower (which he spent writing poetry and compiling a history of the world), he was released to return to the Orinoco in search of gold, now accompanied by his son, Wat. Despite explicit instructions from James I not to attack the Spanish (except in self-defence), some men under Raleigh's command near the Orinoco did just that. Furthermore, his son was killed in the skirmish. On his return, Raleigh had to carry the can – the 1603 treason charge was revived. On 19 October 1618 Sir Walter Raleigh ate a hearty breakfast and took tobacco.

Cavalier and poetic to the last, he refused a blindfold and asked to see the executioner's axe, saying, 'This is a sharp Medicine, but it is a Physician for all Diseases'. His body was buried in nearby St Margaret's, Westminster. As was then the custom, his wife was given his embalmed head. The head was finally buried next to the rest of him. Since Sir Walter's time, Sherborne Castle has been enlarged and modified. Today it is a charming mansion in a lakeside setting, ringed by woods and parkland.

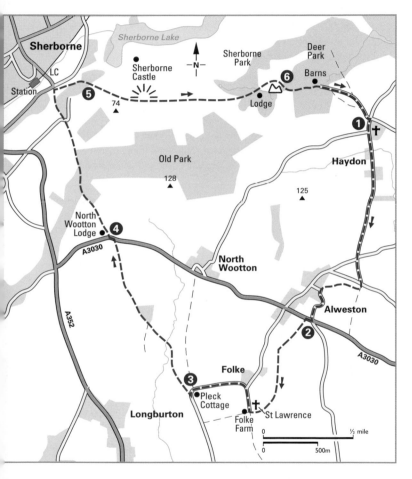

1. With the church on your left, walk down the road and out of Haydon. At the junction continue ahead, signposted 'Bishop's Caundle'. At the minor junction cross the stile, and continue straight ahead. Turn right, up the field-edge, towards Alweston. Cross a stile by a fingerpost and bear diagonally left over the field (if there's a potato crop, or similar, in the field you'll have to skirt around it). Cross a stile in the corner, go down a path and keep straight on down the road, which curves round past a restored pump to meet the A3030.

2. Turn right, and in 30yds (27m) turn left over a stile in the hedge. Go straight over the field to a gap. Bear diagonally right over the next field to cross a stile just to the right of where power lines leave the field. Continue straight ahead to left of the hedge, crossing several stiles and footbridges. Continue along the wall towards Folke church. Cross two stiles, go through a gate, and turn right up the lane into the village, passing the church entrance and a raised pavement on your right. At the junction keep left, by a postbox, then follow the lane as it bends round to the left.

3. Follow the road as it bends left by Pleck Cottage, then turn right up a green lane signed as a bridleway. Follow this for a mile (1.6km), gently ascending. It becomes broader, reaching the main road.

4. Turn left, then right through the gate alongside The Lodge, up a track. This leads down through woods, with the park wall to your right. Where the drive sweeps right by a cottage, keep straight on, down a track, to pass sports fields on your left. Continue through trees, cross a road and go through a kissing gate by a lodge onto a tarmac path. Follow this down a steep valley (formed by centuries of foot erosion) to the main road. Take the path immediately right, through a metal kissing gate, and walk around the slope and above the castle gateway.

5. Pass through a gate into Sherborne Park. Follow the grassy track straight ahead, downhill. Go through a kissing gate and straight ahead on an estate track, with views of the castle. The track runs through a wooden gate to a thatched lodge, and up the hill.

6. At the top keep right, through another gate into woods. Follow the track round. Keep straight on to a concrete path and pass a huge farm shed on your left. Follow the access lane ahead, past a weighbridge, and straight on at the junction. Descend through the lodge gate and straight on to return to your car.

Where to eat and drink
Sherborne has a full range of places, but the Digby Tap in Cooks Lane, near the tourist information centre, is highly recommended as a totally unpretentious ale house, serving real ales and inexpensive bar food. Children are welcome at lunchtime, and you can take your dog inside.

What to see
The battlemented Church of St Lawrence at Folke dates from 1628. If it is locked, walk round and peer through the windows for a sight of the massive carved Jacobean chancel screen.

While you're there
Sherborne is dominated by the huge square tower of the Abbey Church, on Half Moon Street. Admire its sawtooth Norman entrance and outstanding fan-vaulted roof. Exploring the streets on foot you'll find a buttermarket, old yarn mills and a jumble of low houses and little golden terraces, all on a tiny scale. Look out for the lovely Georgian square of Newland Gardens.

ALONG THE STOUR TO FIDDLEFORD

DISTANCE/TIME	5.25 miles (8.4km) / 3hrs
ASCENT/GRADIENT	429ft (131m) / ▲ ▲
PATHS	Grassy paths, muddy woodland tracks, a rutted lane, roadside walking, pavements
LANDSCAPE	Little hills, valleys and settlements of Blackmoor Vale
SUGGESTED MAP	OS Explorer 129 Yeovil & Sherborne
START/FINISH	Grid reference: ST782135
DOG FRIENDLINESS	Some stiles may be difficult
PARKING	Signposted Sturminster Newton Mill, off A357 just west of Old Town Bridge to south of town; also English Heritage car park at Fiddleford Manor for those visiting the building
PUBLIC TOILETS	At Sturminster Newton Mill, open all year

Sturminster Newton consists of two separate entities linked in the 16th century by the Town Bridge. At its heart is the triangular marketplace, dominated by the Swan Inn. William Barnes, a prominent Dorset dialect poet, was born near here in 1801. A newly married Thomas Hardy wrote *The Return of the Native* (1878) during the two years that he lived here, in a house overlooking Newton Mill. In Hardy's novel a despairing Eustacia Vye drowns herself in Shadwater weir. Hardy surely had in mind the thundering waters of the two mills on this walk, which dizzy the senses with their constant roar. Newton Mill, dating from the 17th century, has been restored and can be seen in operation four days a week between April and September.

The tawny buildings of Fiddleford Mill, set amid pollarded willows, poplars and tall reedbeds beside the curving River Stour, create quieter images reminiscent of a Constable painting. The Romans called this place Fitela's Ford, and the mill gets a mention in the Domesday Book of 1086. The mill building itself is tiny compared with Newton Mill. One wall is largely taken up by an inscription from 1566. It exhorts the miller to welcome all comers and to be honest in his dealings. In the 18th century a notorious smuggler called Roger Ridout hid his contraband here.

However, Fiddleford's real treasure lies on the other side of the handsome farmhouse: the remains of the much older and grander Fiddleford Manor, built around 1374 for William Latimer. It came into the family of Thomas White and his wife Ann, who undertook much rebuilding from 1539–55. Their initials appear carved into the tops of the doorways in the passage. The east wing was demolished in the 18th century in favour of a new house, itself demolished in 1956. Abandoned and derelict, the medieval remainder – with its shortened hall – was given to the state and is now in the care of English Heritage. The remarkable little building you walk into today consists of a buttery and passage beside a high-roofed, timbered hall, with stairs leading up to a solar and gallery. The roof beams once supported a flat, moulded ceiling. Now the exposed oak timbers are revealed in all their glory. They are adorned with carved, curved wind braces that have cusps and clover-leaf holes, like the stonework of some sweeping Gothic cathedral. Viewed up close, you can see the paler timbers of restoration, inset in 1980. Work has revealed that the solar room was once painted, and you can see fragments of an angel.

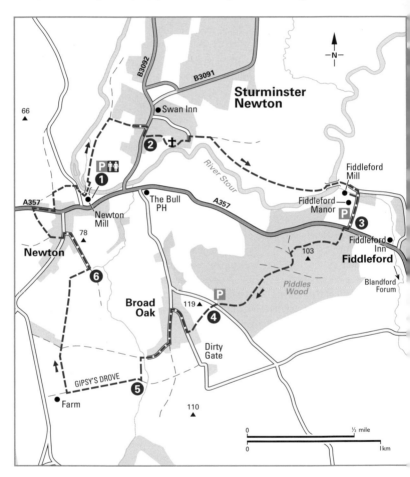

1. Go down steps past the mill, over three bridges and into a field. Keep left up the edge (signed 'Colber Bridge'), parallel with the Stour. Go through a kissing gate and up an avenue of trees marking the end of the playing field. Turn right onto a tarmac path and follow this into and along a lane (marked 'Ricketts Lane' at the far end). Cross the high street and turn right.

2. Turn left by The Old Clock Shop, to walk to the church. Keep to the right of the church, and at the end of the churchyard go through the gate to go down some steps and into a lane. This bends round to the left. Take the path on the right to Fiddleford Manor and Mill. Go through a kissing gate and bear slightly

right over the field, above the river. Go through a kissing gate and bear left along a hedge. Continue straight ahead through another kissing gate. At the far right-hand corner cross two footbridges in quick succession and the mill race, to bear right, past the mill. Go down the drive, turn right and right again through a car park to Fiddleford Manor. Return to the lane and turn right.

3. At the main road turn right then immediately cross to a bridleway, walking straight uphill into Piddles Wood. At the top turn right onto a track and follow it round the hill. Keep forward at two fingerposts and an unmarked crossroads. Take a gate and go through a car park, then go on left to the road.

4. Turn right and immediately left through a farmyard, signed 'Broad Oak'. Go straight ahead through two fields into a lane. At the end turn right along the road, and left at the junction (ignoring Donkey Lane to the right). Follow this road down, soon bearing right. At the end of the road, take the path ahead, and after a footbridge turn left (signed 'Gipsy's Drove') to a stile and along the bottom of a field to cross another stile into woodland.

5. Turn right on the unmade lane – Gipsy's Drove. Follow this for 0.3 miles (480m). Turn right at the top of a rise on a track just before a farm. At the bottom go through a gate and straight over the field and through a solar farm. At the end, bear left then immediately right at a waymarker. Cross a stile, then go straight on along the right edge of the field. Soon cross a stile onto a path. Bear right along a high hedgerow. Continue along a fenced path to a lane.

6. Turn left and, once in Newton, turn left and soon right into Hillcrest Close. Where this bends right, go straight ahead down the lane, signed 'Newton A357'. Climb the stile (by a yellow marker) and continue down the field, with a hedge to your right. Leave via a gate at the bottom, cross the A357 and turn right. After the town sign turn left on a path, signed 'Newton Farm'. After 100yds (90m) bear left and immediately cross a stile on the right. Then bear right to cross another stile. Walk across the field to a stile to the right of a barn. Cross the stile and drop through the woods. Bear right on the road then soon left through a kissing gate. Cross the picnic area to return to the car park.

Where to eat and drink

The pretty Bull at Newton can be reached by a footpath from the mill car park. Alternatively, extend the walk at Fiddleford to the Fiddleford Inn, on the junction with the A357, and enjoy a drink in its garden (no dogs inside).

What to see

Piddles Wood and Broad Oak are part of a nature reserve, which covers 50 acres (20ha) of semi-natural woodland. Look out for the rare wild service tree (*Sorbus torminalis*) with its deeply indented leaves.

While you're there

Seek out the story of dialect poet and parson William Barnes. He attended the little school in Penny Street. He became a solicitor's clerk and a schoolmaster before studying divinity. He taught himself many languages, including French and Hindi. He died in 1886, leaving dozens of poems in the Dorset dialect, which he believed to be the purest form of English.

AROUND TARRANT GUNVILLE

DISTANCE/TIME	5.8 miles (9.3km) / 2hrs 15min
ASCENT/GRADIENT	350ft (107m) / ▲ ▲
PATHS	Field paths and tracks
LANDSCAPE	Rolling farmland and scattered woods
SUGGESTED MAP	OS Explorer 118 Shaftesbury & Cranborne Chase
START/FINISH	Grid reference: ST925128
DOG FRIENDLINESS	Under control
PARKING	Street parking beside village hall in Tarrant Gunville
PUBLIC TOILETS	None on route

Tucked below the slopes of Cranborne Chase, Tarrant Gunville stretches along a narrow lane near the head of the Tarrant valley. The area was traditionally devoted to sheep, the flocks pastured on the higher slopes during the summer and brought to more sheltered meadows during winter, where their droppings provided manure to replenish the soil of the crop fields in the valley. Farming practices have since changed and much of the land is now cultivated, although the wider landscape remains pleasantly broken by small woods and copses.

At the edge of the village, Eastbury Park once surrounded the grandest mansion in the county. Begun in 1718 for George Doddington, Paymaster to the Navy, it was designed by Sir John Vanbrugh, by then already established as architect of Castle Howard and Blenheim Palace. By the time it was completed 20 years later, George was long since dead. The palatial sprawl had cost £140,000, a staggering £25 million or more today, and was too big to manage. It eventually passed to the 2nd Earl Temple of Stowe, who found he couldn't even pay people to live there and (resident in Italy at the time) he gave instructions to his steward William Doggett to dismantle two wings to reduce running costs. Anticipating the Earl would never return, Doggett set about its demolition, selling the materials to improve his own finances. But to his horror the Earl did come home, to find only the stable block still standing. Doggett promptly shot himself – and the Earl, rescuing what he could from the rubble, converted it into the more modest house seen today.

It was taken by Thomas Wedgwood, whose father Josiah had founded the famous Wedgwood pottery. Thomas was a pioneer of photography, devising the concept of a camera. He died in 1805, his ambitions unfulfilled, and is buried in the local churchyard. His brother Josiah II ('Jos') inherited the family business and had moved to Gunville House a year earlier. Jos is credited with introducing bone china, and one of the village lanes is called China Lane. His daughter Emma married her cousin Charles Darwin, whom Jos encouraged to join Captain Robert FitzRoy's second survey expedition aboard the *Beagle*.

The area is rich in prehistoric remains, and the walk passes two Neolithic long barrows which, when excavated in the 18th century, revealed a quantity of human bones. The curious double row of tumuli extending north across the park from Eastbury House are, however, part of an imposing ornamental avenue laid out by the landscape architect Charles Bridgeman in the early 18th century.

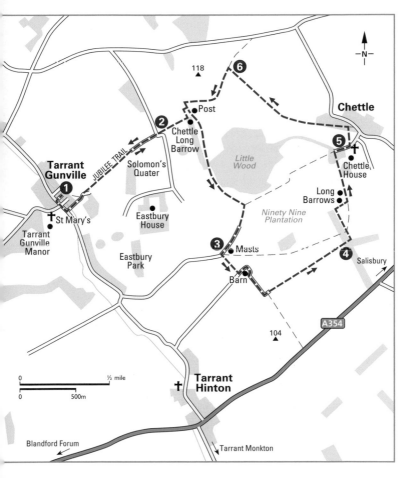

1. Go left along the main street and turn left up School Lane. Where it bends, keep ahead on a track between the houses. At the top, swing right in front of a gate on a path that winds into a wood. Emerging beyond, a fenced path runs on beside an old beech avenue. Through a gate at the end go left and immediately right to continue along a broad track, from which gaps on the right give views of the curious avenue in Solomon's Quarter.

2. At the end, cross a tarred track to a wide gap opposite and continue beside the right-hand hedge. Swing left in the corner to find after a short distance a gate into the adjacent field just beyond an electricity post. Turn right beside Chettle Long Barrow, concealed by an overgrowth of hedge and trees. Walk along the field boundary and continue within the edge of Little Wood. Meeting a crossing track, go right, soon following a belt of trees that hides the ditch

and bank of an ancient earthwork. It is thought to have been associated with a settlement that lay to the east.

3. Just after passing a pair of telecommunications masts, turn left through a metal gate and follow the field edge down to another track. Go left past a barn and then right, immediately bearing left again, with the track. Swing left in the next corner and then keep ahead between open fields for 0.5 mile (800m).

4. Immediately beyond a belt of trees turn left up the field edge and right within the top corner. After 100yds (91m), go through a gap on the left onto a fenced grassy track and walk on past the end of a more obvious long barrow. Leave the field at the top corner to head into trees. Reaching a junction of tracks swing right, dropping past the entrance to Chettle House.

5. Drawing level with the church, look for a fenced path on the left that leads to a farmyard. Curve left along a short track into a field and keep ahead along its length behind the village. Through a gap in the end hedge, bear right along the edge of the next two fields.

6. Passing through a gap at the end, follow a track left. Entering the next field, swing right and then turn left within the corner to find the gate near the electricity post passed on the way out. Retrace your route back to the village.

Where to eat and drink

Although there isn't a pub in the village, you need only go a couple of miles down the lane to Tarrant Monkton where you'll find the 17th-century thatched Langton Arms. It is a traditional country pub with an ever-changing selection of real ales, and has a beer garden and children's play area. It's open every day for food at the bar or fine dining in the Stables Restaurant.

What to see

The charming Queen Anne-style Chettle House, passed as you approach Chettle, was designed in 1710 by Thomas Archer. Described by Pevsner as being 'nationally outstanding as a specimen of English Baroque', the house has no corners.

While you're there

The market town of Blandford Forum suffered a disastrous fire in 1731 and was almost entirely rebuilt to create one of the finest Georgian towns in the country. The work was undertaken over a period of 30 years by the brothers John and William Bastard, whose father had been an architect-builder before them. Particularly impressive is the parish church with its colonnaded aisles and box pews and the corn exchange, which incorporates the town hall. At nearby Blandford Camp, you will find the Royal Signals Museum, which traces the history of the British Army's battlefield communications, from the introduction of the telegraph in the Crimea to cyber-warfare and satellite communications. It is open every day, but situated within the confines of the camp; adults need a valid photo ID to gain entry.

PIMPERNE LONG BARROW AND TARRANT GUNVILLE

DISTANCE/TIME	5 miles (8km) / 2hrs 15min
ASCENT/GRADIENT	360ft (110m) / ▲
PATHS	Quiet country lanes, farm and woodland tracks
LANDSCAPE	Rolling farmland with clumps of deciduous woodland
SUGGESTED MAP	OS Explorer 118 Shaftesbury & Cranborne Chase
START/FINISH	Grid reference: ST925128
DOG FRIENDLINESS	Some road walking
PARKING	Up lane beside village hall in Tarrant Gunville
PUBLIC TOILETS	None on route

The chalk downs of Dorset are littered with the burial mounds of our ancestors. The long barrow on the hill above Pimperne is one of several in the area and marks the site of a Neolithic settlement dating from around 3000 BC. A contemporary earthwork is shown on the OS map, but it has been ploughed into the ground. Down the slope towards the road is a later round barrow, or tumulus. A similar settlement site and earthwork is marked above the Ninety Nine Plantation on a neighbouring slope to the northeast; there are more tumuli here, also disappearing under the plough, and a less impressively preserved long barrow. The settlers in this part of England are believed to have come over from the Continent. They were farmers, introducing cattle and sheep to Britain from southeastern Europe and the Middle East.

Pimperne Long Barrow is one of the best in Dorset. It appears as a 330ft (100m)-long scrub-covered mound at the edge of a field. Long barrows like this were communal graves, usually for men with the status of chiefs and their families. The barrows consisted of mounded earth and stone. There were commonly six to eight bodies inside, sometimes buried with vessels of food and possibly interred over a long period of time. Often, as with the example of the Grey Mare and her Colts, the long barrows were divided into chambers by large, flat slabs of stone. With the fields full of tiny flints, it is easy to see that such luxuries were not available here, and so timber was probably used here. However, the flinty ground was important to the Neolithic settlers for other reasons. A legacy of finely worked spear heads, arrow heads and polished stone axes shows the value of the stone in their lives, both for immediate use and for trading. (There's a good collection in the museum in Dorchester.)

Burial mounds of different sorts are found all over Dorset. The round barrows are probably the most common. They date from around 2000 BC and were usually single graves. Other later forms include the bell barrow, where the mound was surrounded by a ditch, and the bowl barrow, where the body was buried in a crouching position. So-called disc barrows, clearly visible in aerial photographs of nearby Oakley Down, consist of one or two small mounds on a larger circle of flat ground, surrounded by a ditch and bank.

Finds of beads and needles amid the cremated remains suggest these may have been the burial places of high-born women. The construction of barrows continued under the Roman occupation until around AD 750.

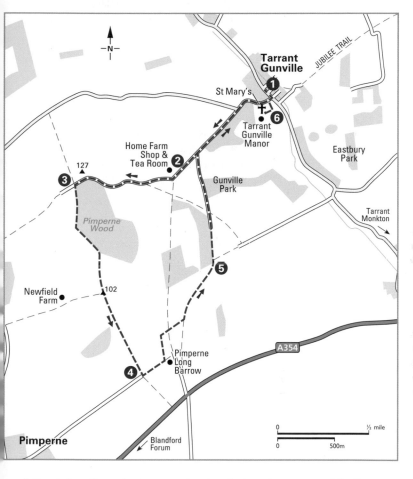

1. Turn left on the main street, passing the telephone box on your right. Turn right by the old forge, signposted 'Everley Hill', and go up the road for 320yds (300m), passing the Manor House gates on the left. At a junction keep ahead following the lane signposted for Home Farm only. After 0.25 miles (400m) keep right at the split.

2. Pass an old farmhouse on the right, with a tiny labourer's cottage in the yard (Home Farm has a shop and tea room close by). At the fingerpost bear right on the track, passing a fine old hedge on the right. Continue gently uphill, passing the end of Pimperne Wood on the left and ignoring two private tracks to the left.

3. At a junction of tracks just over the brow (with a view ahead) turn left on a bridleway along the edge of the wood. At the end of the wood stay on the grass track. Where a farm track drops down to the right, go straight ahead up the

edge of the fields, passing a large concrete block that resembles an outsize Lego brick. As you go over the crest of the hill, the bristling radio mast of Blandford army camp is prominent in the view ahead of you. Beyond rolling Pimperne Down to the right you can see where Hambledon Hill falls away sharply to the north. Continue to where the track meets a metalled farm road.

4. Turn left onto the grassy track, passing a water tower. Go through the gate to Pimperne Long Barrow. Turn left alongside the hedge and right at the sign heading downhill. Then follow the grassy strip between the fields to a track beside the trees.

5. Continue straight on with the trees to the left and, where the track veers to the right, bear left down the edge of the field, passing into the woods at the bottom and continuing up the opposite slope. At the top of the hill, by an overgrown metal gate, go straight ahead down the tree-shaded bridleway. At the track keep left, heading down past some houses to arrive at the junction passed earlier (left leads to Home Farm). Turn right and retrace your steps towards the village of Tarrant Gunville.

6. Before the bottom of the hill, where a path joins from the left, bear right through three gates into the churchyard. Leave the church and go down the path and some steps, turning left at the bottom to a junction. Turn right to continue retracing your steps back into the village.

Where to eat and drink

Beside the church, in the impossibly pretty village of Tarrant Monkton, is the red-brick Langton Arms. Dogs and children are welcome in the public bar. Good food is served all day at weekends, and from 12–2.30pm and 6–8.30pm during the week. The Tea Room at Home Farm, Tarrant Gunville, specialises in home-made cakes and the family-run shop stocks an array of traditional foods.

What to see

A simple marble plaque at St Mary's Church in Tarrant Gunville commemorates Thomas Wedgwood, third son of Josiah, the Staffordshire potter. He died at Eastbury in 1805, aged 34. Thomas's early experiments in photography brought him a small claim to fame – he worked out how to create images, but unfortunately not how to fix them. His elder brother, another Josiah, occupied nearby Gunville Manor.

While you're there

Larmer Tree Gardens at Tollard Royal were planted with an educational purpose by the 19th-century archaeologist Augustus Pitt-Rivers. The larmer tree was an old wych elm, a meeting point for King John and his huntsmen, that blew down in 1894. There's a water garden complete with Roman temple. The gardens are open in summer, Sunday to Thursday, except for July, the end of August and various weeks in September, when music festivals take place.

EXPLORING HAMBLEDON HILL

DISTANCE/TIME	4.5 miles (7.2km) / 3hrs
ASCENT/GRADIENT	541ft (165m) / ▲ ▲
PATHS	Village, green and muddy lanes, bridleways, hillside
LANDSCAPE	Pastoral, dominated by Hambledon Hill, outstanding views
SUGGESTED MAP	OS Explorer 118 Shaftesbury & Cranborne Chase
START/FINISH	Grid reference: ST860124
DOG FRIENDLINESS	Good but some road walking
PARKING	Lay-by opposite St Mary's Church
PUBLIC TOILETS	None on route

The locals would have you believe that you can see America from the top of Hambledon Hill. That's perhaps a little optimistic, but the New World link is not entirely spurious. Lieutenant Colonel (later General) James Wolfe, a veteran of the Jacobite Rebellion in Scotland, trained his troops here for ten weeks in 1756. All that yomping the steep hillsides must have been worth it, for three years later his troops occupied the Plains of Abraham just outside Quebec City and captured Quebec – and subsequently Canada – for the British, although Wolfe himself was mortally wounded in the battle.

The ditches and ramparts of a fort that dates from the Iron Age encircle the top of Hambledon Hill. Today it is acknowledged as a site of international importance for the quality of its rare downland and its archaeology. The platforms of 200 huts have been discovered within the ramparts of the fort, offering a glimpse of how our ancestors lived – it is strange to think of this high, peaceful spot occupied by an entire community.

Such a distinctive landmark as Hambledon Hill was a natural choice for a rallying of serious-minded folk in 1645. They were the local branch of the Dorset Clubmen, ordinary people who were sick of the Civil War, and particularly of being caught in the middle of plundering troops from both sides. Their idea was to declare Dorset a neutral zone until the King and Parliament had sorted out their differences. The King, defeated at the Battle of Naseby earlier in the year, was supportive of the movement. However, to Oliver Cromwell and his fellow commander Thomas Fairfax, it represented a dangerous, obstructive nuisance. When the Clubmen, determined not to be overlooked, tried to cut off Fairfax's supplies as he swept through North Dorset, he seized and imprisoned the ringleaders at Shaftesbury.

On 4 August, some 4,000 angry and ill-armed Clubmen then faced Cromwell and the horsemen of his New Model Army on Hambledon Hill. They suffered a humiliating defeat on their home ground. Around 60 of their number were killed (some accounts say 12), and around 300 were taken prisoner, including four rectors and their curates. Cromwell locked them all up in Shroton church overnight. They were allowed home the next day, after promising not to do it again, and the Dorset Clubmen subsequently disappeared from history. The Parliamentary army stormed on to take Sherborne Castle a few days later, which was another decisive step towards their eventual victory.

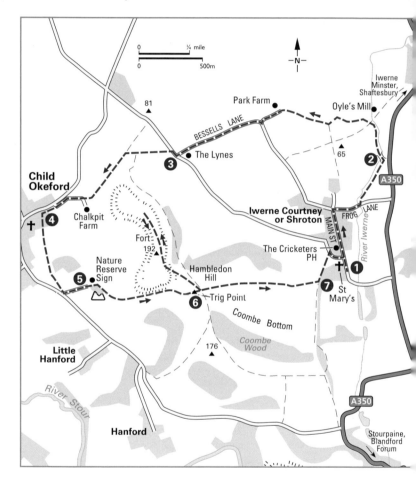

1. With the church on your left, walk up the street. Pass a farmhouse on the corner of Main Street and Frog Lane. Note behind you the carved stone cross, placed in 2000 on the stump of an old cross. Turn right along Frog Lane, and follow it out of the village. Just after crossing the River Iwerne, go left through a gate in the hedge, and walk along the path near the largely unseen stream.

2. Ignore one makeshift footbridge and carry on to cross a more substantial one. Continue to the right along the river then peel off left to aim for the far left-hand corner of the field and go through a bridle gate. Follow the right edge of the next field, with a horribly overgrown footpath below to your right. Pass through a field gate and join this path, going ahead to join it. Thankfully, it is far

less jungly on this section. Ignore field tracks and go through a gate. Pass Park Farm on your right and keep straight ahead. At the junction bear right into an unsigned lane.

3. At the end, by The Lynes, bear right and immediately left up a bridleway, with a line of trees to your left. Keep forward at a junction where the trees end, and at the top bear left down a muddy and narrow track, part of a defensive ditch at the foot of the hill. This joins a drive at Chalkpit Farm and emerges onto a road; turn left and head into Child Okeford. Just past the postbox turn left and go through a kissing gate. Bear right along the edge of the park, towards the church tower. When you get to the fence turn left.

4. Cross the drive via two gates and keep straight on, with glimpses of the chimneys of the Victorian manor house to the left. Ignore a path sweeping away to the right. At the end go through a kissing gate and bear left down a path. Cross a stone stile by the road and immediately turn sharp left up a lane. This becomes a track, climbing steeply through trees.

5. Bear right in front of the nature reserve sign and follow the track uphill. The path levels out below the earthworks that ring the top of the hill. Emerge from the track and continue upwards, following a fence on your left. Where the fence stops, continue upwards in the same direction to the top.

6. At the trig point turn left to explore the ancient settlement. Return to the trig point, turn left over the top of the hill and go down the slope, following the bridleway.

7. Meet a track by a wall at the bottom. Turn left and go through a gate, with the village ahead. Follow the track down to a cricket pavilion. Go through the gate and turn right, onto the road. Follow this down past a barn development and turn right to return to your car. Alternatively, turn left at the pavilion, and soon after turn right by Hill View Cottage, to the pub.

Where to eat and drink
The Cricketers in Shroton is a cosy place. Walkers are requested to leave their muddy boots outside. Dogs are welcome in the beer garden to one side, children inside. The food includes bar meals and baguettes, as well as restaurant fare; there's also a games area.

What to see
Elizabeth Taylor married Thomas Freke, and is remembered as the 17th-century benefactress of the school in Shroton, now the village hall. The family's over-the-top chapel within St Mary's Church was erected by their sons in 1654. It dazzles with its crests and armorial bearings, which some might find rather pompous and florid.

While you're there
Call in at the neighbouring village of Iwerne Minster to admire the church, which dates from the 14th century. Its elegant spire can be seen from the walk. In fact, it is one of only three medieval spires in Dorset. When first built it was apparently twice as tall – restoration in the 19th century cut it down to size.

CHILD OKEFORD AND HAMMOON

DISTANCE/TIME	5.5 miles (8.9km) / 2hrs
ASCENT/GRADIENT	98ft (30m) / ▲
PATHS	Field boundaries, grassy tracks, firm road, grassy bridleways
LANDSCAPE	Open farmland, dominated by Hambledon Hill
SUGGESTED MAP	OS Explorer 129 Yeovil & Sherborne
START/FINISH	Grid reference: ST822120
DOG FRIENDLINESS	Some unfriendly stiles
PARKING	Lay-by on Hayward Lane by old brick railway bridge and Trailway sign
PUBLIC TOILETS	None on route

Child Okeford and Hammoon are just two of the mysterious names of the villages around the green meadows of the Stour Valley. Child Okeford, in the shadow of Hambledon Hill, is one of a triumvirate of Okefords. To the south lies pretty Okeford Fitzpaine, and the nearby quarrying village of Shillingstone was known as Shilling Okeford in the days when it boasted the highest maypole in the country. Hammoon sounds faintly exotic or romantic, but in fact the name comes from William de Moion, a Norman nobleman who was rewarded after the Conquest with a section of low-lying meadowland (or 'hamm'). The family name was later spelt Mohun (which became the 'moon' element of Moonfleet, down by Chesil Beach). The hamlet of golden-brown stone buildings that is clustered round the stump of an old cross is still called Hammoon.

There is more to Hammoon than meets the eye. Tucked behind the church, the venerable Manor Farm is particularly appealing, with tiny windows cut into the deep thatch of its roof and the 17th-century addition of a magnificently carved classical porch complete with grand columns. Next door to Manor Farm is the charming little Church of St Paul's, topped with a weathered, wooden bellcote. Step through the massive oak door into a harmonious interior that is not quite what it seems. Fragments of 13th-century flooring are preserved under the bell tower, but the church is probably another century older. The deeply carved reredos (the screen behind the altar) dates from the late 14th or early 15th century. It was discovered in a builder's yard in London and was installed here in 1946. Another improvement at that time was the addition of the lovely 16th-century choir stalls, carved with flowing vines and grapes – these came from East Anglia.

There's one more surprise on this walk. Ham Down Woodland Burial Ground is on the site of a former vineyard. It is a 'green' burial place where there are no denominational barriers and no weeping statues. Coffins and memorial plaques are required to be strictly biodegradable, and your loved one's grave or scattering place can be marked with the planting of a tree (of an appropriate species for the locality) and a flush of spring bulbs.

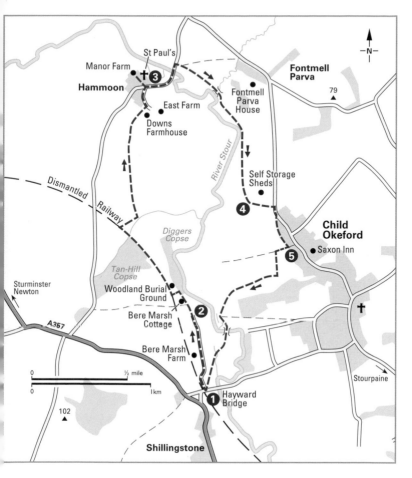

1. Go through the gate and follow blue markers up the farm road, passing Bere Marsh Farm. Pass a house on the left and go straight on through a gate.

2. Just after Bere Marsh Cottage, turn left through a gate, following a sign marked 'Trailway'. Bear to the right of the burial ground, down a broad, grassy ride. Follow this bridleway (blue markers) straight across the fields for a mile (1.6km) to Hammoon. You will pass Diggers Copse on the right and, initially, the bridleway is parallel with the route of a former railway on the left. Turn right at a public bridleway sign to go immediately through a galvanised gate. The route is now straight ahead, though you will have to skirt round the field-edges if the fields are planted. After the fifth gate pass Downs Farmhouse. The track becomes a road. Bend left then right to emerge opposite the stump of an ancient cross. Cross over to look at Hammoon's church and walk up the lane to admire the (private) Manor Farm.

3. Return to the main road and turn left. After crossing the weir climb a concrete stile on the right. Head across the field bearing right, away from the treeline, to meet the river. Cross a footbridge over a stream at the end of the field and look ahead for a glimpse of the red-brick Fontmell Parva House.

Go diagonally right across the field to a gateway in the corner by the river (yellow marker) then bear right along the edge of the field, above the river. Go through another gate and after 400yds (365m) along the right-hand edge of the field, turn left to a line of trees. Follow waymarked directions along the right side of the trees, with self-storage sheds visible behind those to your left.

4. At the corner of the field go through a gate and down the lane. At the road turn right into Child Okeford (the Saxon Inn is further down here, on the left). At Mulberry House (just past the Bower turning sign) turn right and immediately follow the direction of a white wooden arrow in the grass on the left to access a path between wooden railings. Walk down an enclosed path, behind some houses, to go through a galvanised gate into a field. Continue along the left edge, go through another gate, and head along a path behind hedges.

5. Emerge at a lane and turn right. Soon turn left at a gate and follow a path between fences, then cross a field to four gates close together, keeping to the right side of a stream. Walk along the left edge of the field, go through a gateway and keep straight on. Go through two more gates then, ignoring a half-left path that leads to a footbridge in a copse, bear diagonally left in line with distant buildings across the field to reach a raised footbridge, high above the water. Cross this concrete bridge and keep straight on towards a bridge in the hedge. Cross over and bear left to the corner of the field, to return to the start.

Where to eat and drink

The Saxon Inn in Child Okeford is tucked away, off the main road. It's part of a second row of houses and easy to miss if you're hurrying through the village. It offers home-made food and a beer garden. Families and dogs are welcome.

What to see

The multiple chimneys of Fontmell Parva (a private house) are glimpsed through the trees on this walk and there's a better view of this curious old house from the road into Child Okeford. Built of red brick and crowned with a hipped roof, it dates from 1670 and is characterised by the arched mouldings over its windows, which seem to give the house a look of surprise.

While you're there

On the other side of Hod Hill, the village of Stourpaine is worth a look. You'll have to turn down off the main road by the White Horse Inn (apparently built on the side of the old octagonal toll house) to see the best of it. Cob cottages sit snugly under thatched roofs, and a pleasing church boasts a medieval tower. The curved roof on the back of Coalport Cottage is unusual.

HOD HILL AND HAMBLEDON HILL

DISTANCE/TIME	5 miles (8km) / 2hrs 15min
ASCENT/GRADIENT	970ft (296m) / ▲ ▲
PATHS	Field tracks and paths
LANDSCAPE	Steeply rolling farmland
SUGGESTED MAP	OS Explorer 118 Shaftesbury & Cranborne Chase
START/FINISH	Grid reference: ST853112
DOG FRIENDLINESS	On leads near grazing livestock
PARKING	Small car park (free) beside minor road north of Hod Hill
PUBLIC TOILETS	None on route

An irregular triangle of high ground overlooks the confluence of the River Iwerne with the Stour, their valleys splendidly isolating it from the downs on either side. There are actually two separate tops divided by a deep saddle, imposing a double ascent on any walk linking the two. But the climb is amply repaid in the rewards of spectacular views and the chance to explore two of Dorset's most impressive hill-forts.

Such sites exist across the country and were traditionally regarded as purpose-built 'forts', used as refuges during unrest. However, the eventual realisation that most contained significant numbers of dwellings suggests transhumance or even permanent settlement, despite the lack of water on the hilltops.

By the 1st century BC, the area was held by the Durotriges, Celtic farmers well versed in the manufacture of pottery and ironwork and who traded with the Continent through a port at Hengistbury Head. The Roman invasion in AD 43 brought a sudden end to their way of life – for, despite a strong resistance, they were eventually conquered and lost their identity.

Hod Hill

The settlement on Hod Hill is perhaps the easier to interpret; a large, roughly rectangular earthwork containing some 54 acres (22 hectares), the largest such enclosure in Dorset. It is defended on three sides by a double bank and ditch, while the steeper slope overlooking the Stour has only a single bank.

In the southeast corner are traces of round houses and enclosures, and it is estimated that there were around 250 families led by a chieftain. When the Romans arrived, he appears to have been the focus of attack, as a concentration of ballista bolts was found during excavation around the largest hut. But the absence of buried war dead suggests the settlement might have surrendered in the face of such force. The Romans established their own fort in the northeast corner, its outlines still clearly visible. The remains of the commander's house, storehouses, latrines and a water tank have been identified.

Hambledon Hill

The earthworks on Hambledon Hill originated during the Neolithic period and were successively extended into the Iron Age, culminating in an extensive triple bank. A long barrow and the foundation platforms of around 200 huts have been identified, but it is thought the site was largely abandoned by around 300 BC, in favour of Hod Hill. The hillsides are lightly managed by grazing and occasional scrub clearance to encourage a wide range of wild flowers. These in turn attract butterflies, including several blues and the grizzled and dingy skippers.

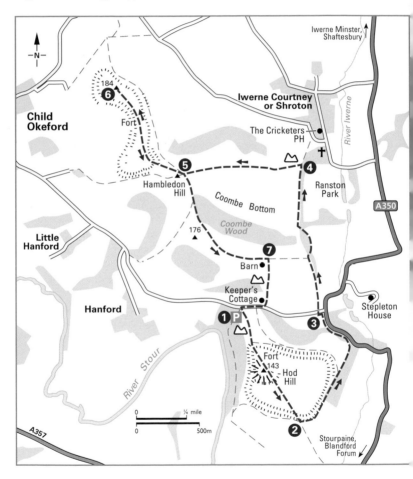

1. Of the several paths radiating behind the car park, take the one climbing left to a gate into the bottom corner of a field. Do not follow a sign to Hod Hill, but bear half right to climb beside the edge of a wood. Beyond a gate at the top, the path breaks through the ramparts and continues diagonally across a vast enclosure. Partway, it cuts through a lower earthwork, the boundary of the Roman fort sited in its northwest corner.

2. Reaching the far corner, drop through the defences towards a gate and stile. Turn left immediately before it on a path below the ramparts. A short way along turn through a gate to a chalk track below. To the left, it gently descends across the slope of the hill to end through a gate onto the main road. However, instead of passing through, bear left on a bridleway above the road. Pass through a gate into a field and head down to a gate near the bottom corner.

3. Cross a lane to another gate almost opposite and climb away at the right field edge over the shoulder of the hill. Where the hedge swings left, go through a waymarked gap on your right. Follow a path through scrub wood, passing through a second gate to descend above a bank of coppiced hazel. Meeting a gravel track at the bottom, go left and then right across the foot of Coombe Bottom. Behind the railings on the right is Ranston Park. Climb to a junction on the shoulder of the hill.

4. The track ahead leads down to Iwerne Courtney, where you will find a pub in the village. The onward route, however, is to the left, climbing steadily along the ridge to a trig point marking the highest point of Hambledon Hill.

5. The survey column stands at the centre of a Neolithic camp, but the much larger Iron Age fort lies to the right beyond a shallow saddle, straddling the more extensive northern arm of the hill. The multiple embankments and ditches of the fortification snake around the upper slopes and you can easily spend an hour or more wandering around the site. The views are particularly impressive when the sun is low.

6. Return to the trig column and walk ahead along the ridge, gradually descending to a gate. Curve left above the top of Coombe Wood and continue with the broad, descending ridge towards a barn, going through a gate along the way.

7. Pass through a gate and swing right with the track, the gradient steepening as it falls into the valley. At the bottom, emerge onto a lane beside Keeper's Cottage. Turn right back to the car park, keeping a watchful eye for traffic.

Where to eat and drink

The Cricketers at the foot of Hambledon Hill is a cosy place serving local beers as well as lunch and dinner. Choices range from home-made soup and a baguette to full restaurant fare, with Sunday roasts and a changing specials board. Dogs are welcome in the beer garden, but please take off muddy boots before going inside.

What to see

Keep an eye or better still an ear open for the green bush cricket, which can grow to 2in (50mm) long and is Britain's largest insect.

While you're there

Upstream along the Stour valley just outside Sturminster Newton you will find Fiddleford Manor, a delightful 14th-century house on the banks of the river. It is now owned by English Heritage and is open to the public daily all year round (free entry). Inside, fine carved stonework and intricate timber roofs are particularly impressive.

GUSSAGE ST MICHAEL AND THE DORSET CURSUS

DISTANCE/TIME	5.25 miles (8.4km) / 2hrs 30min
ASCENT/GRADIENT	295ft (90m) / ▲
PATHS	Firm tracks and green lanes (muddy after rain), sections of road
LANDSCAPE	Arable farmland and pasture dotted with ancient remains
SUGGESTED MAP	OS Explorer 118 Shaftesbury & Cranborne Chase
START/FINISH	Grid reference: ST986115
DOG FRIENDLINESS	Leads required through farmyards; some road walking
PARKING	Lay-by in lane opposite garage, by entrance to Lower Farm, Gussage St Michael
PUBLIC TOILETS	None on route

Like many parts of Dorset, the eastern vales offer some lovely views and are littered with ancient remains that add a touch of historical interest to any walk; the area around Gussage St Michael is no exception. The small, sprawling village is squeezed between Ackling Dyke, an important Roman road, and a more ancient, processional way known as the Dorset Cursus. There are two more Gussage villages to discover: the larger All Saints to the southeast and the tiny Gussage St Andrew to the northwest. The curious name shared by the three villages is derived from the Saxon words for a spring ('gyse' for 'water breaking forth') and 'sic' meaning a watercourse; the second part of each name is derived from the dedication of the local church.

The Cursus is a broad track, between parallel banks and ditches, some 6 miles (10km) long, running across this northeast corner of Dorset from Bokerley Dyke to a cluster of long barrows and tumuli. It appears to be aligned with the rising and setting sun at midsummer and midwinter. Its edges have been blurred by time and the plough, but one of the clearest sections can be seen on this walk. It's believed to date to Neolithic times, around 2000 BC, but its purpose isn't clear. There are some great views northwards from Gussage Hill over Gussage Down. You can see the shadow of the parallel ditches of the Cursus heading away towards Pentridge and Penbury Knoll, marked by a clump of dark firs. Hollows and hummocks on the flank of Gussage Hill suggest the remains of a large Neolithic settlement, and the top is liberally scattered with tumuli and long barrows. Towards the end of the day the low light of the setting sun makes the ground shimmer silver with cobwebs.

Slightly more recent is the former Roman road of Ackling Dyke. This major route can still be traced for 22 miles (35km) between Old Sarum (near Salisbury), which had links to London, along the Portway and the hill-fort at Badbury Rings from where a Roman road continued to Dorchester. The return part of the walk follows a section of this former Roman road.

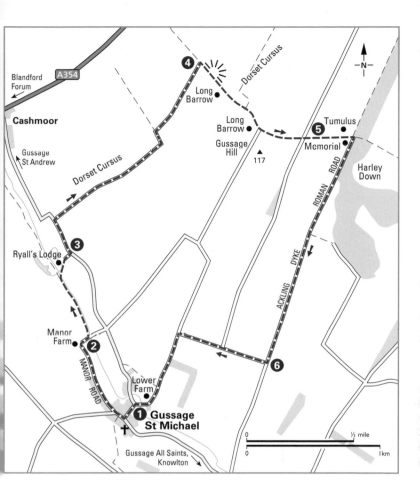

1. Turn left down the street in Gussage St Michael, as if you were going to the church, but turn right by Corner Cottage, onto the road signposted to Long Crichel. Where the road swings up to the left, go straight on, into Manor Road, following the footpath sign for Cashmoor. Continue along the broad green valley, passing houses on the left. Go past the large gates (path opening on the left side) and continue along the driveway.

2. At Manor Farm turn right down the drive for 100m and then left across a stile beside a gate. Follow the track for 0.25 miles (400m), until you are level with a clump of trees to the left. Cross a stile to your right, then a footbridge and another stile. Bear left across the field corner to a footbridge into a garden. Turn sharp right through the garden to cross a stone footbridge and pass between the houses and garages at Ryall's Lodge. Go up a drive to a road.

3. Turn left along the lane for 320yds (300m) and, after passing a house (Meadowside) on your left, turn right on a surfaced track (bridleway), running parallel with the Dorset Cursus to your left. Continue past some farm buildings and stay on the track as it kinks left across the Cursus then bends right up the hill to a gate at the top.

4. Turn right along the grassy fence-lined bridleway. Follow this for slightly under a mile (1.6km) along the ridge of Gussage Hill, with views northwards over Gussage Down and ancient long barrows and tumuli to the right. Keep straight ahead at the intersection of tracks near the top of Gussage Hill, passing the trig point over to your right and a ragged line of hawthorn bushes.

5. Follow the bridleway into the trees to a junction, passing an unexpectedly modern memorial stone to one John Ironmonger, who died in 1986, and turn right along the track. The walk now follows the former Roman road (Ackling Dyke) for slightly over a mile (1.6km), first with woods to the left and then between hedges; the dyke is raised at this point, with a ditch and bank to the right.

6. At a barn on the left turn right on a droving track between high hedges. Keep straight on along the wide gravel track to a T-junction and turn down to the left. Later pass the buildings of Lower Farm. Bear right along the lane beside an old flint wall with tile cap on the right, crossing a stream to return to the lay-by where you started.

Where to eat and drink

The Drovers Inn at nearby Gussage All Saints has a good-sized garden and welcomes children and dogs. The interior is pleasant and airy, with light oak tables, old beams and a bright, modern bar. The pub has won awards for its real ales and its meals are cooked using locally produced ingredients, including vegetables from its own garden.

What to see

Dorset originally provided a vast acreage of unfenced grazing for sheep. The flocks would be moved around via a network of broad, hedged droving lanes, many of which still exist. Often with a profusion of wild flowers and sometimes overgrown, they provide ideal walking tracks today and are identified by the old names, such as Dancing Drove and Sweetbriar Lane.

While you're there

The ruin of Knowlton church, set just off the B3078, is a curiosity well worth a visit. It sits in splendid isolation at the centre of a circular henge with a ritual significance that is now lost. A church was first erected here in Norman times, but there is no sign of the village that it once served – that disappeared centuries ago, wiped out by the plague. Today the grassy bank is smothered with wild flowers and butterflies, making it a peaceful spot for a picnic.

CHALBURY HILL AND HORTON

DISTANCE/TIME	4.5 miles (7.2km) / 1hr 45min
ASCENT/GRADIENT	400ft (122m) / ▲ ▲
PATHS	Field paths and tracks, some lane
LANDSCAPE	Gently rolling farmland
SUGGESTED MAP	OS Explorer 118 Shaftesbury & Cranborne Chase
START/FINISH	Grid reference: SU032074
DOG FRIENDLINESS	Dogs on leads near grazing livestock
PARKING	Lay-by near village hall, on eastern edge of Horton
PUBLIC TOILETS	None on route

This walk wanders through a landscape of rolling pastures and fields broken by copses and woodland, and links quiet villages that each have something of interest. Horton is where James Scott, 1st Duke of Monmouth, was captured in 1685 after his army's bloody defeat at the Battle of Sedgemoor. Although the eldest son of Charles II, he had been denied the succession because of his illegitimacy. But his ill-fated rebellion to wrest the throne from his uncle, James II, ended with his beheading on Tower Hill.

The village's unusual L-shaped 18th-century church stands on the site of a 10th-century Benedictine abbey dedicated to St Wolfrida, a Saxon noblewoman who became abbess of the nunnery at Wilton Abbey. The tiny whitewashed church at nearby Chalbury is one of the oldest in Dorset, and the simple beauty of its exterior is repeated inside. Box pews for gentry farmers face a fine three-decker pulpit, while elevated behind a balustrade in the chancel is a bench for the Earl of Pembroke. All is overlooked by a musician's gallery. Nearby on the high point of the hill stood a telegraph semaphore, part of a chain employed by the admiralty to transmit signals between Plymouth and Whitehall during the Napoleonic Wars.

Hinton Martell was originally Hinetone, the village of the monks, and the present church was rebuilt following a fire during the 19th century, with the architect-turned-novelist Thomas Hardy working on the plans. Incorporating the old stones, it retains the Early English style and includes a sundial on the tower. At the other end of the village is a striking fountain, more in keeping with the formal gardens of a grand house. Originally installed around 1875 by William Burt, owner of a paper mill at Witchampton, it served as a pressure relief for the village's newly installed water supply. The present centrepiece is the third replacement, a replica of the original cast-iron cupid.

The walk finishes past Horton Tower, otherwise known as Sturt's Folly, which, when built in 1750, was the country's tallest secular building. Humphrey Sturt, lord of the manor, was both an architect and the county's MP as well as a keen huntsman, and it is said that he constructed the tower to watch the hunt when too old to ride. That he was then only 25 shows commendable retirement planning, but it might merely have been an observatory for viewing the night sky. Although derelict inside, it now serves as a mobile phone mast.

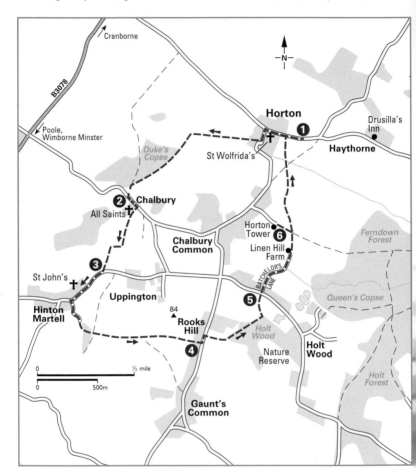

1. Walk through the village to a junction by the Old School House and go left towards Chalbury Common and Wimborne. Just past St Wolfrida's churchyard, leave over a stile on the right between two house drives. At the end, go left and right over a stile and head across pasture past an old chalk pit. Go through a gap in the hedge, stepping over a low metal stile. Continue by the right-hand hedge of the next field. Over two more stiles, immediately strike out left across the field towards Duke's Copse. Crossing another stile, bear right to a gate at the corner of the wood and walk up beside the trees. Through a metal field gate to your right, angle across a final field towards the most right-hand of a clutch of houses and follow a track out to a lane.

2. Go left but almost immediately bear off on a footpath to Chalbury's church. Pass through the churchyard to leave by a kissing gate and stile opposite the

south porch. Head diagonally right down the field to a stile, swinging left before it onto a fenced path beside a fringe of trees. Go through a gate on your right and over a stile to emerge in another field. Walk down by the right-hand hedge, swinging left at the bottom towards stables. Go over a stile to pass behind them along a contained path to a track and go right and left to a lane.

3. Walk downhill into Hinton Martell, passing the church to a junction by an unusual village pond. Go left towards Rooks Hill, skirting a high fence to reach the corner of a wood. Turn in on a narrow path winding up into the trees. Keep right at a fork near the top. Continue forward along the left-hand hedge of successive fields, crossing several stiles and eventually leaving along a short track onto a lane at Rooks Hill.

4. Turn left and immediately right on a gravel track, passing through a gap at its end into Holt Wood. Fork left, crossing a footbridge over a stream, and keep left at the next junction to reach a crossing green track. Go left again, shortly exiting past a barrier onto a gravel drive. Follow it out to meet another lane.

5. Cross to Batchelor's Lane opposite, following the track to Linen Hill Farm. As it swings sharply left behind the buildings, keep ahead over a stile into a field. Bear left uphill to a stile in the top boundary by an electricity post. Follow the track left to have closer look at Horton Tower.

6. Return to the electricity post and go over the stile on the left. Drop diagonally across the slope towards the houses at Horton, passing the end of a concrete track to a stile at the far side. Keep going, crossing four further stiles in quick succession and a final field. Emerge over a stile beside a gate next to the canopied village pump. The lay-by is then just to the right.

Where to eat and drink

Just along the lane towards Wigbeth, Drusilla's Inn exudes old-world charm and is open daily, serving lunchtime and evening food that ranges from ploughman's and burgers to full three-course dinners and Sunday roasts. There's a children's menu, and well-behaved dogs are permitted in the bar.

What to see

The route passes through Holt Wood, a corner of the Holt Heath National Nature Reserve, here an area of thick woodland characterised by oak, beech and holly managed by pollarding and grazing. The reserve extends east as lowland heath, which attracts many birds such as the nightjar and Dartford warbler. It is the only place in Dorset where curlews breed and is home to all six of Britain's reptiles.

While you're there

The National Trust's Kingston Lacy is only 5 miles (8km) to the southwest, a magnificent country house set within an extensive park. Among its treasures is the collection of Egyptian antiquities amassed by William Bankes during his 19th-century eastern travels. Nearby are the Badbury Rings, an impressive Iron Age fort that crowns a low hilltop and whose banks are covered in wild flowers that include many orchids.

AROUND HORTON

DISTANCE/TIME	7.5 miles (12.1km) / 4hrs
ASCENT/GRADIENT	690ft (210m) / ▲ ▲
PATHS	Field paths, tracks, some road
LANDSCAPE	Gently rolling farmland, mixed woodland
SUGGESTED MAP	OS Explorer 118 Shaftesbury & Cranborne Chase
START/FINISH	Grid reference: SU032074
DOG FRIENDLINESS	On lead on road sections
PARKING	Lay-by with phone box beside the village hall, just east of Horton
PUBLIC TOILETS	None on route

The countryside around Horton holds a sad reminder of a flamboyant rebel, who was captured here after being discovered asleep in a ditch below an ash tree. On 11 June 1685, James, Duke of Monmouth, the illegitimate son of the late King Charles II, landed from exile in Holland at Lyme Regis. West Dorset was a base for anti-Catholic dissenters, and on earlier visits the Duke had been warmly greeted with cries of 'God bless the Protestant Duke, and the Devil take the Pope'. He believed he could raise enough support in the West Country to claim the throne from his uncle, the Catholic James II.

Accompanied by a small band of supporters, Monmouth set about recruiting. He announced that he had come to defend the Protestant religion and to deliver the country from the tyranny of James II. Within a few days his following had grown to 4,000. At Taunton, Monmouth had himself declared King. On 6 July the rebels clashed with James II's forces at Sedgemoor in Somerset. The battle was over in 90 minutes, with a loss of 16 of the King's men and some 300 rebels. The Duke was forced to flee.

He hoped to escape on foot, disguised as a local shepherd, through the county of Dorset to the coast at Poole, where he could board a ship. However, rewards were posted, and the countryside quickly filled with troops seeking the rebel leader. The Duke and a companion, a German named Buyse, fled across the fields of Horton Heath, but were spotted climbing a hedge by an old woman who told the authorities. Buyse was soon captured, and a few hours later militiaman Henry Parkin discovered another exhausted figure. A search of his pockets disclosed the badge of the Knight of the Garter, and golden guineas revealing that this was no shepherd. Monmouth was taken to London and was beheaded on 15 July.

The repercussions of the failed rebellion were felt hard in Dorset. The brutal Lord Chief Justice Jeffreys was put in charge of the trials of 312 of Monmouth's supporters in what became known as the 'Bloody Assizes' at Dorchester. Most were transported to the colonies, but 74 were executed, their bodies publicly mutilated and hung on display.

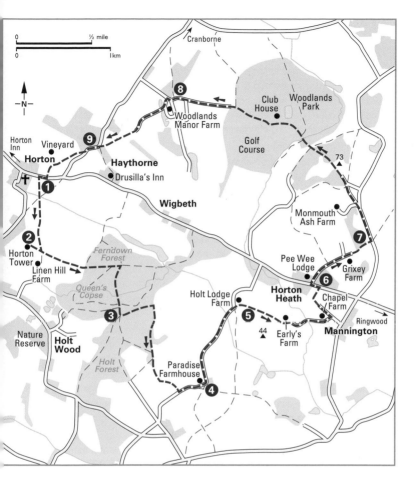

1. Go towards the village, turn left over the stile by the pump and head towards Horton Tower, crossing five more stiles in quick succession. Go up the hill, bearing diagonally left. Cross the fence at the top corner and turn right for the tower, which stands 140ft (42m) high.

2. Retrace your steps from the tower and stay on the track heading downhill, and go through a gate into Ferndown Forest (Priors Copse). After 275yds (250m) bear left (straight on) onto a firmer track for 110yds (100m) and turn right at the marker post. Keep ahead (southwards) through Queen's Copse, later crossing a stream and a track to reach a wooden barrier.

3. Pass this barrier, go through an earth bank and immediately turn left following the bank and ditch on your left. Turn right just before the edge of the wood, and follow the path for 0.75 miles (1.2km). Bear left at the split (marker post) to a track and turn left, following the track through a gate to reach Paradise Farmhouse.

4. Turn left along the track between the two houses and follow it towards Holt Lodge Farm. At the cross junction turn right and follow the track as it curves

left. After 160yds (150m), where the track curves left, go straight on between the fence (left) and hedge (right) following a 'public footpath' sign. Unfortunately, the path can become clogged with nettles.

5. Keep straight ahead to cross a stile, and turn immediately left to a gate at Early's Farm. Turn right in front of the house and follow the track for 0.25 miles (400m). At a T-junction after Chapel Farm, turn left (signed to 'The Longhouse') and, where the track bends left in front of a gate, go right over a stile. Bear left around the field, cross another stile behind a house and continue to the road.

6. Turn left, and just before Pee Wee Lodge turn right along the track. Keep straight on at the junction (left heads for Horton Heath Farm), then fork right to Grixey Farm. Follow the waymarker uphill, crossing three stiles, and bear right to a field then left up alongside the copse on the left to a stile.

7. Turn left along the track for 0.25 miles (400m) and bear left, signed 'Monmouth Ash Farm', and take the bridleway to the right of the house. Keep straight on and at the split take the left bridleway up over a sandy heath (disused pits) and down into woodland, which is now home to Remedy Oak Golf Club. Keep right at a green metal gate in front of a small brick building. At the split (marker post) fork left to pass the clubhouse and continue along the metalled road; later you can see Horton Tower.

8. Walk to the right of the golf club gates and turn left towards Woodlands Manor Farm. Cross the stile and fork right towards Greenlands Farm along a metalled track with a fence on the left. At the junction bear down to the right between two lakes and stay on this road. After it becomes a track, look for a yellow marker on the right pointing to the other side of the hedge, just after the farm. On the far side, go diagonally across the field to two stiles. Bear right to the corner of the next field. Go past a gate and turn right to meet the road.

9. Turn left through Haythorne but, just after the 'Horton' sign and before the road starts descending, go right through trees to a gateway and follow the enclosed path downhill to emerge by the vineyard. Turn left along the track and left again to return to your car.

Where to eat and drink
On the main road 0.5 miles (800m) east of Horton is Drusilla's Inn, a pub with a thatched roof, real ales and a fabulous view over to Horton Tower. To experience Horton pie, try the Horton Inn, northwest of the village.

What to see
Horton Tower stands like a giant rocket-launcher on its hilltop. The 140ft (42m) tower was built by Humphrey Sturt in 1762 as an 'observatory'.

While you're there
On the B3078 just to the north of Horton sit the ruins of medieval Knowlton Church. What makes these particular ruins spectacular is that they are right in the midst of a much older construction – a large prehistoric henge, which forms part of a concentration of local Neolotihic and Bronze Age structures. The church and henge are free to look at and open during daylight hours.

OVER THE DOWNS TO TURNWORTH

DISTANCE/TIME	4.5 miles (7.2km) / 2hrs 30min
ASCENT/GRADIENT	155ft (47m) / ▲ ▲
PATHS	Flinty tracks, bridleways, forest paths, village road
LANDSCAPE	Farmed valleys, expansive views, windswept chalk ridge, woodland
SUGGESTED MAP	OS Explorer 117 Cerne Abbas & Bere Regis
START/FINISH	Grid reference: ST812093
DOG FRIENDLINESS	Beware of horses
PARKING	Okeford Hill car park and picnic area (very narrow entrance) just west of the road, at the top of hill north of Turnworth; more accessible lay-by further north, on opposite side
PUBLIC TOILETS	None on route

Though Thomas Hardy (1840–1928) is well known as a novelist and a poet, his first chosen career as an architect is barely acknowledged. Hardy was born at Higher Bockhampton into a family of builders and stonemasons, so it was natural enough that at 16 he should start architectural studies as a trainee draughtsman with John Hicks in Dorchester. In 1862 he moved to London, where he specialised in church restoration work. Returning to Dorset five years later, Hardy continued with intermittent architectural work, initially working again on church restoration projects for G R Crickmay in Weymouth.

The church of St Mary in Turnworth, which you'll pass, is an example of this type of work. Hardy was responsible for the design of the carved stone foliage for the church's pillars, although the work was actually carried out later. His most visible and best-known architectural achievement is his own house at Max Gate, Dorchester, a large Victorian villa, started in 1885, which is a tenanted National Trust property, open to the public from April to September.

Thomas Hardy used his native county as the background for his books, setting his stories in varied and vividly described settings all over Dorset. Many of his books feature downlands, of which Turnworth is one, and many of these upland pastures are probably among the least altered by modern agriculture. Dorset downs are still used for grazing, and it's the constant cropping of the grass by sheep that keeps rampant growth under control and makes the downs home to a wonderful range of beautiful, chalk-loving wild flower species. Depending on the time of year you choose to walk, look out for springtime cowslips in huge numbers, with bluebells in the woods that often border the downs. Summer sees a succession of wild native orchids, tiny intricate flowers whose names describe them – greater butterfly, common spotted, pyramidal, bee and fragrant. In midsummer wild thyme scents whole hillsides, and it's followed by yellow and gold bird's foot trefoil, heady wild mignonette – nothing to look at but highly scented – and the tiny, jewel-like autumn gentian. These all attract butterflies, moths and insects galore, while the short-cropped turf makes a perfect nesting site for skylarks, which you'll hear high overhead long before you see them.

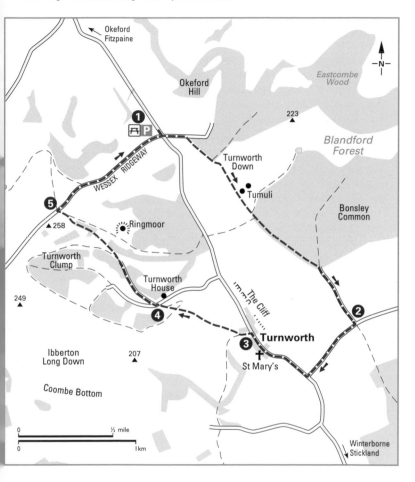

1. Turn right out of the picnic area and down the hill, almost immediately turning left down a wide track. About 250yds (230m) on – just after a green barrier in front of a wood and just before a Forestry Commission sign for Okeford Hill – fork right. Follow this woodland path for about 0.25 miles (400m), then bear right through a gap by a yellow footpath marker and immediately turn left along a broad green ride, with a windswept hedge on your left. Go straight on, following the track as it runs through woodland, descending gently and narrowing all the time to the end of the wood. Stay on what has become a narrow path between hedges with open farmland beyond for 0.25 miles (400m).

2. At a crossroads of tracks, marked by a fingerpost, turn right. The path leads downhill, passing a barn on the right. At the bottom turn right and walk along the road to Turnworth village, passing the Church of St Mary on the left.

3. After house No. 10, avoid a bridleway on the left, but take the next bridleway on the left 50yds (45m) later. Soon enter a field and go diagonally right, passing left of the nearest clump of trees. At the top corner go through a gateway and keep on straight, bearing diagonally left across the field through a gap in the left-hand hedgerow. Continue on this line, bearing right across the corner of the field under a great oak tree, to reach a stile in the fence. Cross this and bear diagonally left down the steep hill. Below, on the right, you will see Turnworth House and its park and walled garden. Cross a track and keep going down, to reach a gate above a barn. Go through it and walk round to a road. Turn left and immediately right opposite Okeden House.

4. Go through a gate on the right and head up the steep road. Tarmac soon gives way to track. The track soon curls left round the top of the woods. Bear diagonally right, up the flinty field, aiming for a gap in the hedge to the right of a low metal trough. Bear left along a grassy track between two hedgerows. The track narrows to a path and leads to a kissing gate. Go through this and turn left up the edge of the field. The ridges and ditches to your right are signs of an Iron Age farming settlement – this is Ringmoor (owned by the National Trust). Pass the extremely overgrown ruins of a farm on your left and reach a gate. Go through this, pass a pond and go through another gate.

5. Turn right onto the Wessex Ridgeway path – signed 'Okeford Hill' – and follow this for 0.75 miles (1.2km), gently downhill with outstanding views to the northwest. Just before the road turn left through a gap in the hedge to re-enter the picnic area.

Where to eat and drink

On the main street of Okeford Fitzpaine, you'll find the old Royal Oak. It's open lunchtimes and evenings and it offers changing specials, as well as a beer garden. Dogs are welcome in the bar with its massive beamed inglenook fireplace. Children are welcome in the lounge bar.

What to see

In St Mary's Church at Turnworth look for an unusual memorial stone in the north aisle, inscribed with barely decipherable Latin text. The translation tells that John Straight, a 17th-century vicar, was determined to have a memorial to himself created during his lifetime, to record his success in reclaiming massive back-taxes for the church.

While you're there

Beacons lit up the skies along the line of the Wessex Ridgeway to warn of the Spanish Armada in 1588, notably on Melbury Hill. The event was commemorated with a line of fires in July 1988, when the great beacon was raised on Okeford Hill. Reach it from the bridleway near the lay-by just north of the starting point. The view is, of course, superb.

IBBERTON AND THE WESSEX RIDGEWAY

DISTANCE/TIME	4.25 miles (6.8km) / 2hrs
ASCENT/GRADIENT	591ft (180m) / ▲▲
PATHS	Quiet roads, muddy bridleways, field paths
LANDSCAPE	Edge of steep escarpment with views over Blackmoor Vale
SUGGESTED MAP	OS Explorer 117 Cerne Abbas & Bere Regis
START/FINISH	Grid reference: ST792072
DOG FRIENDLINESS	Lots of road walking may be tiring for soft paws
PARKING	Car park at Ibberton Hill picnic site
PUBLIC TOILETS	None on route

The Wessex Ridgeway is a long-distance footpath that runs for 137 miles (220km) from Marlborough in Wiltshire across Dorset to Lyme Regis. The 62 miles (100km) of the Dorset section start at the high point of Ashmore. Although it was only completed in 1980, the path follows much older routes across the hills and downs. This walk uses a good stretch of it, on the chalk ridge between Okeford Hill and Bulbarrow Hill.

The view from the Ridgeway at this point is captivating. You're 902ft (275m) above sea level and from the viewing table you can identify the distant Blackdown and Quantock hills to the left, the symmetrical mound of Glastonbury Tor ahead, and, to your right, Shaftesbury and Cranborne Chase. Immediately below, the patchwork fields of Blackmoor Vale are spread out in shades of green and brown, with clumps of trees and scattered dwellings and farms. Even today they are the little communities, linked by hedges and lanes, which Thomas Hardy captured so well in his novels and poetry.

Tucked under the hill and spreading up its flank, Ibberton is a particular delight, a blend of stone, flint and thatch, with old and new houses side by side. The church is somewhere very special. One of only three in the country dedicated to St Eustace, it sits high above the village and has an enviable view over the valley. Its grey stone is silvered with lichen and the wall by the door leans alarmingly. Inside there is a tranquil atmosphere of light and space. Fragments of medieval glass splash gold in the otherwise plain leaded windows. There are no pews, but wooden chairs are ranged around, suggesting that this is a well-used community space. Faded photographs show the church in a state of collapse during rebuilding in 1901. There was a wooden gallery still in existence around that time. A hollowed-out millstone was once the only font. The memorial to a young man killed in World War I is on a touchingly human scale too, with a tiny painted portrait hanging on a pillar. He was Charles Hugh Plowman, the rector's younger son. He died in far-off Macedonia, leaving no mortal remains to be returned to his grieving family. With three other villagers, he is also remembered on the war memorial – the church clock. The villagers are right – it's a remarkable place.

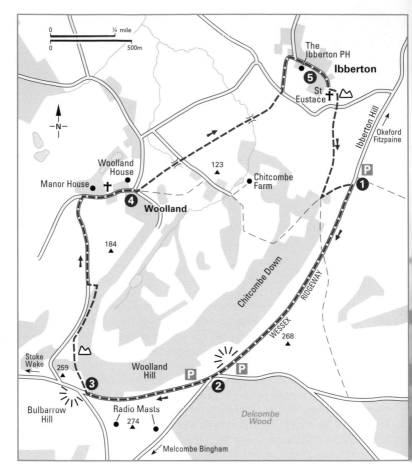

1. From the picnic site car park, turn left along the road, following the route of the Wessex Ridgeway, with the village of Ibberton laid out below you to the right. The road climbs gradually, and you will see the masts on Bulbarrow Hill ahead.

2. After a mile (1.6km) pass a car park on the left, with a Blackmoor Vale and Woodland Hill information board. At a junction bear right and immediately right again. Pass another car park on the right. The woods of Woolland Hill now fall away steeply on your right. Pass the radio masts to your left and reach a small gate into a field on your right, near the end of the wood. Before taking it, go the extra few steps to the road junction ahead for a wonderful view of the escarpment stretching away to the west.

3. Go through the gate and follow the uneven bridleway down. Glimpse a spring-fed lake through the trees on the right. At the bottom of the field swing left to a gate. Go through this onto a road. Turn right, continuing downhill. Follow the road into Woolland, passing the Manor House and the Old School House.

4. Just beyond the entrance to Woolland House on the left, turn right into a lane and immediately left through a kissing gate. The path immediately forks. Take the left-hand track, down through some marshy patches and a stand of young sycamores. Posts with yellow footpath waymarkers lead straight on across the meadow, with gorse-clad Chitcombe Down up to the right. Cross a small quagmire and a footbridge over the stream. Go straight on to cross a road. Keeping straight on, go over a stile in the hedge. Bear left down an uncomfortably overgrown enclosed path – arm yourself with a stick if possible and cross a stile to continue down. Cross a footbridge and go through a gate to continue along the left side of the next field. Go through a gate to a road junction. Walk straight up the road ahead and follow it right, into Ibberton. Bear right to reach The Ibberton pub.

5. Continue up this road through the village. It steepens and becomes a path, bearing right. There are some steps that lead up to the church. Continue up the steep and stony path, which may be treacherous in heavy rain. Cross the road and go straight ahead through the gate. Keep straight on along a fence, climbing steadily. Cross under some power lines, continue in the same direction, still climbing. Carry on up a large area of open pasture, to a small gate in the hedge. Do not go through the gate, but turn sharp left, up the slope. There's no footpath to speak of, so skirt to the left of the trees above you and then aim for a small metal gate. This will bring you onto the road opposite the car park.

Where to eat and drink

The 16th-century pub The Ibberton (at Ibberton) has a magnificent flagstone floor inside and sunny beer gardens outside that possess their own enchanting brook. The pub's ancient, studded oak door opens to the tantalising smell of good food and the welcoming sight of an inglenook fireplace. Dogs are allowed on leads in the garden and in certain areas indoors.

What to see

The waymarker for the Wessex Ridgeway is a green-and-white disc showing a two-legged, winged dragon called a wyvern, which is a symbol associated with the ancient kingdom of Wessex. The path reflects the route of an ancient, much longer highway called the Great Ridgeway that was once used to transport goods between Devon and the north Norfolk coast.

While you're there

Explore Ibberton more thoroughly by picking up a leaflet for the village's Millennium Path – you'll find them freely available in the pub and the church. The 2.25-mile (3.6km) pink-waymarked route takes you around the back lanes between the cottages. Stiles have been replaced by gates to make the going easier.

MELBURY LOOP

DISTANCE/TIME	6 miles (9.7km) / 3hrs
ASCENT/GRADIENT	656ft (200m) / ▲ ▲ ▲
PATHS	Village lanes, estate tracks, farmland paths
LANDSCAPE	Hills, valleys and parkland
SUGGESTED MAP	OS Explorer 117 Cerne Abbas & Bere Regis
START/FINISH	Grid reference: ST574077
DOG FRIENDLINESS	Keep dogs on leads in the park of Melbury House; some lifting over stiles may be necessary and there may be temporary electric fences
PARKING	By church, Melbury Osmond, signed off A37
PUBLIC TOILETS	None on route

Melbury comes from two Old English words: 'maele', meaning multicoloured, and 'burh', meaning a fortified settlement. The three settlements may well be pre-Norman: Melbury Osmond is listed in the Domesday Book (1086). This first Melbury is a typical Dorset village. In Thomas Hardy's *The Woodlanders* (1887) Melbury Osmond, his mother's home village, is called 'Little Hintock', and is described as 'snipped out of the woodland'; 'such a small place that, as a town gentleman, you'd need to have a candle and lantern to find it if ye don't know where 'tis'.

Melbury House (private) is part of the Ilchester Estate. It was built around 1550, in Ham Stone from Ham Hill just across the Somerset border – the golden stone that gives so much character to Dorset and Somerset villages and manors. The glazed tower, with windows all round the upper level, pokes above a roof punctuated by tall chimney stacks and pointed gables. It stands in a park where fallow deer roam, contained by the fences and cattle grids passed through on this walk.

Bubb is perhaps the prettiest Melbury of them all. The hamlet has a small but handsome Jacobean manor house, partly hidden behind its stone garden wall. On the other side of the track stands a wooden granary on staddle stones. The church has a barrel roof, and some fine stained glass dating back to 1474, which is when the tower was rebuilt, though other parts are more recent. The church is heated by a wood-burning stove and lit by oil lamps. The font to the left of the door is strongly carved with deer, hounds, dragons and other beasts intertwined with foliage. Oddly, it's upside down and tapers the wrong way – it is probably a recycled part of an 11th-century Saxon cross. The valley of the River Wriggle is believed to be the line of the pre-Roman Ridgeway track, so a Saxon settlement here is not unlikely. After leaving Melbury Bubb you pass St Edwold's Church, one of England's smallest churches. The 30ft by 12ft (9m by 11m) building dates from 1636, though the odd little bell turret is Georgian. St Edwold, a hermit, lived at Cerne in the 9th century. For more details see *Tiny Churches* by Dixe Wills (AA Publishing).

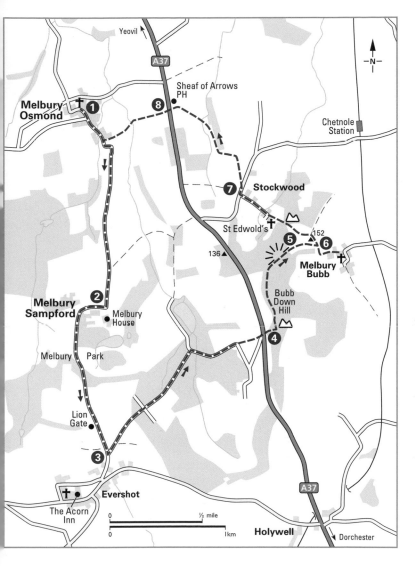

1. Walk down the street, cross the watersplash, and follow the road up past Townsend Dairy House. Across a cattle grid, take the straight estate road for almost a mile (1.6km) to Melbury House.

2. Before the house, at a cattle grid, turn right along the road around the outbuildings. It bends left over a cattle grid, then runs for another 0.75 miles (1.2km) through the park, up and over a hill. Cross a stile by a lion gateway.

3. With Evershot in sight ahead, hook back to the left on a tarmac track, which becomes gravel. Follow this up the hill. Where it divides, take the track straight ahead downhill, past a plantation on your right. At the foot of the slope, turn right. The track curves left and starts to rise. Where the wood on your right runs out, bear slightly left up the field, to a small gate into woodland. Follow the path ahead through the wood to the A37.

4. Carefully cross to the bridleway gate ahead. Follow a path up through the wood, then turn left along an earth track. Soon an open field can be seen below. Go straight across one gravel track for just 70yds (65m), to turn right on a second gravel track (Murderers Lane) beyond. It winds up to the wood edge and a great view northwards.

5. Keep straight ahead down the field, to the right of the trig point, and turn right along the hedge behind. Through a ramshackle gate, turn down left to Melbury Bubb. Use two gates to go through a farmyard. Follow the lane right to explore the church.

6. Retrace your route up to the trig point. Bend left around it and contour above two steep little combes, then drop right. Cross a stile in the corner just left of power lines. Walk along rotting duckboards through boggy woodland, cross a stile into a field and bear left, joining a gravel farm track. Access to St Edwold's is over a brick-built bridge to your left. Pass Church Farm to your left, and bear right up its access track to a road.

7. Turn right on the road, then immediately left, through a gate into a field. Turn right and walk along the hedge. Cross two stiles and bear left down the next field. About halfway down, bear left over two stiles in a hedge. Turn right along the field edge, then left up the field end to a footbridge in the hedge, almost swallowed up by vegetation. The right of way continues the same line but is often planted over; in which case, turn right along two sides of the field to take a mud track up left to the A37 at the Sheaf of Arrows.

8. Turn left along the verge, then cross to a stile just before JVS car showroom. Keep ahead along the hedge. At the field end go through a gateway and turn left over a footbridge and a stile. Bear half right up the field, and aim towards a triple-gabled stone house, crossing a drive and going through a hedge gap. Take the gate to the left of the house, and walk on to the road by the watersplash. Turn right to return to the church.

Where to eat and drink

On the A37, on the walk route, is the newly refurbished Sheaf of Arrows. The pub used to be called the Rest and Welcome Inn but a former landlord, Paul Conway, discovered that the hostelry was used by Thomas Hardy as the Sheaf of Arrows in his 1884 tale, *Interlopers at the Knap*. The pub serves home-cooked food and real ales. There's an extensive beer garden and children's play area.

What to see

Thomas Hardy's mother, Jemima, was born in Melbury Osmond in what is now 1 Barnhill Cottages. She married his father, Thomas, in the church here. Hardy used the village as 'Little Hintock' in *The Woodlanders*, with Melbury House identifiable as 'King's Hintock Court'.

While you're there

The high street in Evershot, with cute bow-fronted shops and a bakery, is an unusual sight in this part of the world. The Acorn Inn, which features in Hardy's *Tess of the D'Urbervilles*, serves local produce.

THE MONARCH'S WAY THROUGH WINYARD'S GAP

22

DISTANCE/TIME	3.25 miles (5.3km) / 1hr 30min
ASCENT/GRADIENT	410ft (125m) / ▲ ▲
PATHS	Field paths, some roads
LANDSCAPE	Little hills and valleys around a high ridge
SUGGESTED MAP	OS Explorer 117 Cerne Abbas & Bere Regis
START/FINISH	Grid reference: ST491060
DOG FRIENDLINESS	Generally good but some road walking can be a bit tiring
PARKING	Lay-by north of Cheddington, opposite Court Farm by a National Trust sign for Winyard's Gap
PUBLIC TOILETS	None on route

In 1651 the rightful claimant to the English throne found himself on the run in Dorset. Charles II had been making for the coast, but was chased back inland. Forced to take a longer route via Yeovil and Mottisfont, he eventually reached Shoreham, where he could catch a ship to exile on the Continent. Charles had an unfortunate inheritance. In 1649, his father, Charles I, was the first and only British monarch to be executed. The young Charles had fought in early battles of the Civil War, but had been packed off to Europe when it became clear that things might not go the King's way. (Part of his exile was spent in Jersey, where his illegitimate son James, Duke of Monmouth, was born.

The Scots proclaimed the young prince King, and invited him home. On 1 January 1651 he was crowned Charles II at Scone Palace. However, the English Parliament was not going to give up power that easily. At the Battle of Worcester that September, Cromwell's army triumphed, and Charles had to flee. It was another nine years before the mood of the country changed and the 'Merry Monarch' could be invited back to take up his throne.

From Worcester Charles fled south through the Cotswolds, reaching the home of the Wyndham family at Trent, on the north Dorset border, where he went into hiding. From here a ship was arranged to take him to France. The King was to rendezvous with the skipper, Stephen Limbry, at the Queens Head pub in Charmouth, disguised as the servant to an eloping couple. Things did not go to plan. Charles was a wanted man and his description had been widely posted. Limbry's wife became suspicious and, fearing that her husband might be captured, locked him in his bedroom. When the captain failed to show up, Charles moved boldly on to Bridport, escaping from there by a whisker. He made his way back to the Wyndhams via Broadwindsor and holed up for another 12 days, before a second attempt to reach a ship was successful. Today the route of Charles II's flight is commemorated with a long-distance path called the Monarch's Way, which leads through Winyard's Gap. It is ironic that his father had come the same way at the head of an army and in a much more bombastic mood seven years earlier while campaigning in Dorset.

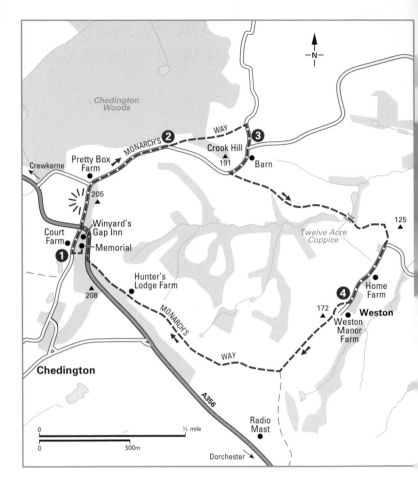

1. Go through the gate at the back of the lay-by. Keep left, then turn up steps to the 43rd Wessex memorial. Return to the lay-by, and turn right along the road. Pass the Winyard's Gap Inn on your right then, at the junction, cross straight over and walk up the minor road ahead. Sweeping views open out to the west. Keep right, following the lane over the top of the ridge between shoulder-high banks – the sign of an ancient lane. Flat-topped, bracken-clad Crook Hill is ahead. About 0.25 miles (400m) after the lane junction, bear left through a gate, signposted 'Monarch's Way'.

2. Go along the field parallel with the top edge of Chedington Woods, which fall steeply away on the left. Go through a dilapidated gate on the right-hand side of the clearing and bear right through the woods, round the base of Crook Hill, which is up on your right. Cross a stile and bear diagonally left down the field towards the right-hand corner of a wood. The marshy area can be avoided by skirting round to the right of it, along a low fence. On reaching a farm road, turn right. Follow it up to meet the lane and turn right.

3. After 200 yards (180m), on a corner, go left through a gate and hook back down the fence on your left. Go through two gates at the bottom and continue

down the field, alongside the top hedge then slightly below it. Twelve Acre Coppice, down to the right, is a lovely stretch of mixed woodland. At the bottom, go through a field gate and cross the stream via a bridge, then go straight ahead up the track. Pass through a gate and keep ahead across a field. Go through another gate, this one with a round water tank beside it, to pass left of a barn, and turn right on the farm road, through Home Farm Dairy. At the lane go straight ahead, passing Home Farm on the left, into the hamlet of Weston.

4. Just before Weston Manor Farm bypass it by turning right through a gate (blue marker). Rejoin the track beyond the farm, as it heads straight up the hill, with a radio mast topping the ridge ahead. After a short tunnel of trees bear right through a gate along a green track, part of the Monarch's Way. Stay on the track through two gates. Pass the gravestone of a local woman – the epitaph upon it is well worth stopping to read. Soon pass through a gate and then another to the left of a barn, with ponds down to the right. Walk above Hunter's Lodge Farm and up its drive to the road. Turn right on the main road and follow it, with care, down to Winyard's Gap Inn. Turn left here to return to the lay-by and your car.

Where to eat and drink

Walkers receive a friendly welcome at the Winyard's Gap Inn. It's a typical Dorset country pub, with home-cooked, locally sourced food, real ales and a skittle alley. Children are welcome in the family room and dogs in the bar, or you can dine out on the terrace in front of the view.

What to see

On the hilltop above the Winyard's Gap Inn is a large carved stone memorial to men of the 43rd Wessex Division. It is dedicated to the memory of all ranks who laid down their lives for the cause of freedom during World War II, and is a replica of that erected on Hill 112 near Caen, in Normandy, site of the first major battle in which the division took part, in July 1944.

While you're there

Take a stroll down the road into Chedington, enjoying the superb views over to the west. The village is a mixture of pretty stone houses and thatched cottages, with a large timbered village hall. The mellow red sandstone church is now a house, called Old St James. If you walk down far enough you'll even find the village pump, by the old police cottage.

FORDE ABBEY AND THE VALLEY OF THE AXE

DISTANCE/TIME	5 miles (8km) / 2hrs 30min
ASCENT/GRADIENT	443ft (135m) / ▲
PATHS	Little-used field-edges and paths, country lanes
LANDSCAPE	Tranquil, broad, fertile valley
SUGGESTED MAP	AA Walker's Map 11 Lyme Bay
START/FINISH	Grid reference: ST376033
DOG FRIENDLINESS	Keep on lead along roads
PARKING	By church in Thorncombe village centre
PUBLIC TOILETS	None on route

You will reach the village of Thorncombe along some of the narrowest lanes in Dorset. Go slowly and carefully along them, for signposting is erratic here, visibility is limited to the next bend, and you really don't want to miss anything.

You could start to believe that few visitors have penetrated this charming quarter. You'd be mistaken, though, for a famous gem of Dorset heritage lies this way. It is difficult to imagine now that the majestic buildings of Forde Abbey lay abandoned for almost a century, after the then 400-year-old Cistercian monastery was closed down in 1539. (The initials 'T C' of the abbot Thomas Chard may still be seen on the oriel windows of the great, square entrance tower.) The splendid ruins of the abbey were bought in 1649 by Edmund Prideaux, who rose to become Attorney General to Oliver Cromwell.

Prideaux's priority was to make a family home, and to achieve this he shortened the Great Hall, turned the chapter house into a private chapel and remodelled the monks' gallery into a saloon. The wonderful garlanded plasterwork ceilings date from this time. Prideaux's reputation and finances were severely damaged, however, after his son entertained the rebel Duke of Monmouth here in 1680; a hefty fine was levied on the estate after Monmouth's defeat at the Battle of Sedgemoor in Somerset. Vivid Mortlake tapestries depicting the Acts of the Apostles, which hang in the saloon, were presented by Queen Anne to the then owner, her Secretary of War, Sir Francis Gwyn.

However, it's the setting of the abbey within its spectacular gardens that is really the most memorable thing. Take time to linger and view the clipped specimen yews and deep beds of summer flowers across the still waters of the Long Pond. Add to all of that a kitchen garden, stunning herbaceous borders, a rock garden (created from old gravel workings) and a bog garden. It's open all year round, with drifts of snowdrops lining the approach in early spring and even an arboretum for autumn colour. Dog owners will be pleased that, providing they are kept on a short lead, dogs are actually welcome here.

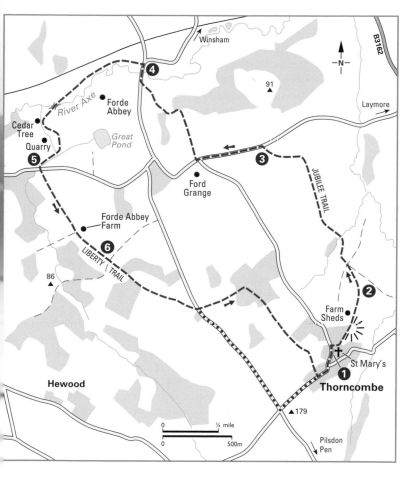

1. With the church on your right, follow the road, then take a signposted path on the right through the second part of the churchyard. Bear right on the lane and immediately left before some garages. Cross the road by Goose Cottage. Go through a gate and follow the top edge of two fields, passing farm sheds on your left, then go straight on down the hedge.

2. Cross a stile in the corner and go straight across the field to a kissing gate – from here to Forde Abbey, you'll mostly follow 'Jubilee Trail' roundels. Through the gate bear right, down to the far corner of the field (not the obvious hedge gap). Cross a plank bridge and then a small stream, and bear left, up the field-edge as it bends right. Go through a galvanised gate on the left, and continue up to the right. Soon go through a gate and follow a path between fence and hedge, then go through a kissing gate and turn left along the field-edge. After a gateway gap turn left through another small gate and go ahead up the field-edge to a gate. Bear right, to the left of a hidden house, onto a road.

3. Turn left for 500yds (460m) to a junction. Opposite the side road on the left, turn right and head straight down (west of north) to woods on a wide grassy path that splits the field. Turn left at a marker along the front edge of the

woods, and at their corner go right, through a gate by a stile. Go down across a small stream, and turn right (northwest) to cross a field diagonally to a hidden gate at the far corner. This leads onto the road opposite the gates of Forde Abbey. Turn right to cross the River Axe. In another 100yds (90m) there's a fingerpost ('Horseshoe Road') and a stile on the left.

4. Follow the footpath round past the back of the abbey. At the far corner cross a footbridge over the River Axe and bear right past a lone cedar. Bear left up to cross a stile, marked 'Liberty Trail'. Walk along the top of the woods to another stile and bear left on a fenced track around a newly opened quarry. Bear right at the junction with a track to go around the back of the quarry to a road.

5. Go straight across, and head up the right-hand edge of the large field. Towards the top right-hand corner bear right through a gate under a power pole, then keep on this new direction along the top edge. Cross a pair of stiles and go through a rusty kissing gate in the corner, pass Forde Abbey Farm on your left and keep straight on to the right of the hedge. Cross a stile on the left to join the tarmac farm road.

6. At a junction of tracks keep straight on. Where the track ends, bear left through a gateway and head up across the field (east) to a gate in the far corner. Cross the road beyond to take a signed footpath, and head straight across the field (north of east) to some woodland. (If this field path is over-planted with crops, you can follow the Liberty Trail, which uses the minor roads to Thorncombe.) Aim for a gap in the hedge and follow the main path ahead through the coppice, keeping forward into denser woodland then gradually bending round to the right (southeast). Emerge by a stile into a field, and keep ahead along the left edge of two fields. Halfway into the third field, where houses begin, go through a gate on the left and continue ahead on an enclosed path to Thorncombe, passing a couple of shortcuts to the church to your left. Turn left on the village street, and left again to the church.

Where to eat and drink

Though only accessible to those visiting Forde Abbey, the very attractive Undercroft Tearoom is open all year (11–4.30). Much of the food served comes from the abbey's kitchen garden. It is licensed, specialising in local cider, and dogs are welcome. If you want to put a picnic together, however, you can always visit Thorncombe's village shop, which sells snacks, fruit and veg, and ice cream.

What to see

Look into St Mary's Church at Thorncombe for two 15th-century brasses, memorials to Sir Thomas and Lady Joan Brook.

While you're there

For many years, the boast of Pilsdon Pen was that, at 909ft (277m), it was the highest hill in Dorset. It's a pity, then, that when nearby Lewesdon Hill was remeasured using modern techniques, it was found to be 2m (6ft) higher than Pilsdon Pen's summit. It's still a very fine hill, despite the demotion. To the southeast of Thorncombe, it is topped by an ancient fort and affords extensive views south.

MINTERNE MAGNA AND HERMITAGE

DISTANCE/TIME	6.7 miles (10.8km) / 2hrs 45min
ASCENT/GRADIENT	1,014ft (309m) / ▲ ▲
PATHS	Tracks, woodland and field paths (not always clear), some lanes
LANDSCAPE	Rolling farm and woodland
SUGGESTED MAP	OS Explorer 117 Cerne Abbas & Bere Regis
START/FINISH	Grid reference: ST659043
DOG FRIENDLINESS	Dogs on leads near grazing livestock
PARKING	Car park (free) opposite church at Minterne Magna
PUBLIC TOILETS	None on route

Often overlooked by those heading to the giant at Cerne Abbas, Minterne Magna is a delightful hamlet centred on a tiny church and fine manor house. It looks across the head of a peaceful valley in which the River Cerne springs, to the long ridge of Minterne Hill, while just to the north overlooking Hermitage is Telegraph Hill, the fourth highest in the county.

As its name suggests, Telegraph Hill was the site of one of the admiralty shutter telegraphs, a system designed by Lord Murray in 1795 to relay messages over long distances. The first link was set up between London and Deal and soon extended to the naval bases at Portsmouth and Plymouth. The stations were set at roughly 7-mile (11.3km) intervals, and a short message could be sent and acknowledged over 400 miles (644km) in less than 10 minutes. The semaphores were mounted above wooden huts that housed the operators and were used until the end of the Napoleonic Wars.

Originally a manor to Cerne Abbey, Minterne House was bought by John Churchill at the beginning of the 17th century. His son Winston left the estate not to his eldest son, John, the Duke of Marlborough (from whom Winston Churchill was descended), but to his younger son, Charles. On his death the house was sold to Admiral Robert Digby (a descendant of Sir Everard Digby, executed for his part in the Gunpowder Plot), who began landscaping the gardens. The original house succumbed to dry rot and was rebuilt in 1905 in the Elizabethan style by Leonard Stokes, a founder of the Arts and Crafts movement. The gardens, laid out in a horseshoe, incorporate waterfalls and lakes and are particularly noted for their rhododendrons and azaleas.

At the other end of the walk is Hermitage, tucked away in the fold of the valley and described at the turn of the century by Edward VII's surgeon, Sir Frederick Treves, as being 'a Rip Van Winkle village'. The name derives from its settlement in the 12th century by a small group of Augustinian friars. They had gone by the middle of the 15th century but left behind the tiny church. It has been renovated several times since, the attractive barrelled roof being installed around 1800 along with the bell turret.

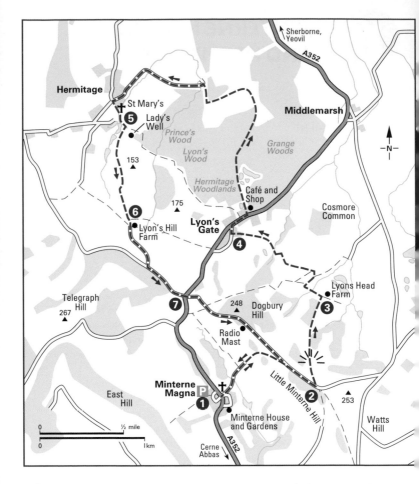

1. Opposite the car park, a track leaving beside the church drops across the River Cerne to climb Little Minterne Hill. Where it later swings right, bear left through a gate and continue up between fields. Beyond a second gate, slant uphill to the right, go through a gate and bear right again at a signpost. Follow the ridge track right for 0.25 mile (400m) to a bend.

2. Through gates on the left, strike half left across open pasture, enjoying the expansive view north over lush farmland. Shortly heading downhill, continue between fences, dropping beyond to join another track that leads on to Lyons Head Farm.

3. At the house, turn left on a metalled track. As it swings right to wooden gates, keep ahead to step across a stream to reach a stile and gate. Climb by the right hedge to a gate at the top. Go immediately through a second gate on the right, a contained path that leads past rough plantation to open pasture. Meeting a track, follow it left uphill. Leave the track at a plantation corner to head straight forwards up and over a field (there's no path) to a hedge gap. Bear right to find a gate at the far side into trees. Drop over a slowly rotting footbridge to an overgrown pasture. Climb away half right and through a gap in a bramble bank to find a gate, hidden towards the right-hand end of the top boundary. There is no path here and you'll have to forge your own way across this abandoned pasture. When you do find the gate, you'll have to push through brambles to reach it. Entering a rough field, go left through a hedge gap and strike diagonally down to go through two field gates below stables.

4. Emerging onto a lane at Lyon's Gate, go right and then right again along the main road. After 150yds (137m), cross to a track into Hermitage Woodlands. At a bridleway sign a short way along, go left over a footbridge and through a wood. Walk through the trees to a footbridge and gate. Emerging into a field, bear diagonally left to cross it to a gate in the top-left corner with a yellow footpath arrow. Follow the right-hand field-edge, swinging right with the hedge to a field gate. Go through it and along a short track to a metalled lane. Turn left, passing Williford Farm. Follow the lane into Hermitage, turning left at a T-junction by a postbox. A few paces later, turn left along a footpath to a gate on your right, passing along a gravel path to the Church of St Mary. Go through a kissing gate into the churchyard. After exploring the church, leave by a metal gate to the right of the church porch.

5. After passing through a garden, turn left along a signed footpath, passing to the left of a pond. Go through a gate to enter a field, leaving through a gap part-way up the right hedge. Cross two fields, then climb across the slope in the third field to a stile in the top right corner. Go immediately over a second stile and follow the right-hand field-edge, climbing to another pair of stiles.

6. Follow the field-edge to a field gate on your right. Pass through it, with Lyon's Hill farmhouse to your left, to go up an obvious track leading uphill, and bearing left. Climb ahead past the farmhouse and out to a lane. Turn left down to the main road.

7. Cross to a track opposite, which climbs onto Dogbury Hill. Walk on past a transmitter mast along the high ridge above Minterne Magna for another 0.25 mile (400m) to find the gate through which you came up. Retrace your outward route back to the car park.

Where to eat and drink
Cerne Abbas was a centre of brewing. During the 18th century it had 17 taverns and was 'more famous for its beer than any other place in the kingdom'. There's only three to choose from today, but they offer everything from a light snack to fine dining. There's a café and small shop at the Lyons Gate campsite.

What to see
Walk through Minterne Gardens, which blossoms from spring through to summer and is then noted for its fine autumn colour.

While you're there
Head down the valley to Cerne Abbas and its Giant, but wander around the village too. It has many pretty buildings, an interesting church with traces of a 14th-century wall painting, and a magnificent tithe barn.

THE CERNE ABBAS GIANT AND MINTERNE MAGNA

DISTANCE/TIME	5.5 miles (8.8km) / 2hrs 30min
ASCENT/GRADIENT	591ft (180m) / ▲ ▲
PATHS	Country paths and tracks, minor road, main road
LANDSCAPE	Head of Cerne Valley, scattered with old settlements
SUGGESTED MAP	OS Explorer 117 Cerne Abbas & Bere Regis
START/FINISH	Grid reference: ST659043
DOG FRIENDLINESS	Lead essential on road stretches
PARKING	Car park (free) opposite church in Minterne Magna
PUBLIC TOILETS	Cerne Abbas

The chalk outline of the Cerne Abbas Giant is so familiar that the reality, seen from the hillside opposite rather than above from the air, is a surprise. His proportions change at this shallower angle, and this of course is how he was designed to be seen – all 180ft (55m) of him. Quite when he was made, and by whom, is a mystery. Was he drawn by the Romans, a portrait of the demi-god Hercules? Could he be a post-medieval caricature of Oliver Cromwell? On the other hand he might be of Celtic origin, for the giant has been linked to a pan handle discovered 12 miles (19km) away on Hod Hill. Made of bronze, it depicts a naked man clutching a club in one hand and a limp hare in the other. The man has wings and is surrounded by other symbols that identify him as Nodens, a Celtic god of healing and fertility. His features and the angle of his legs resemble the Giant, and place him in the first century AD. The Giant has been seen as a symbol of fertility for centuries.

The fencing now around him is to prevent him from being eroded. St Augustine visited Cerne and preached to the locals on the spot now marked by St Augustine's Well. A notice on the wall there records how he offered two shepherds the choice of beer or water to drink. When they primly asked for water, the saint rewarded them with a brewery. An abbey was founded here in AD 987. Its most famous inhabitant, Aelfric, produced a number of schoolbooks in Anglo-Saxon. A Latin primer, in which pupils adopt the characters of working people, and describe their lives to their teacher, is a fascinating record of daily life. The abbey was dissolved in 1539, along with Dorset's other monastic houses, but an imposing gatehouse with an overhanging oriel window and carved lions remains, along with other buildings, including an ancient hospital, set around a flowered courtyard. The village of Cerne Abbas is a lovely mixture of old houses, some half-timbered, some stone, with flint, thatch and brick in evidence. The Red Lion Hotel – now known (doubtless with an eye on the tourist trade) as The Giant Inn – claims to be one of 13 original public houses, and if that seems excessive in a place this size, it should be explained that Cerne was once a major staging post on the coaching routes.

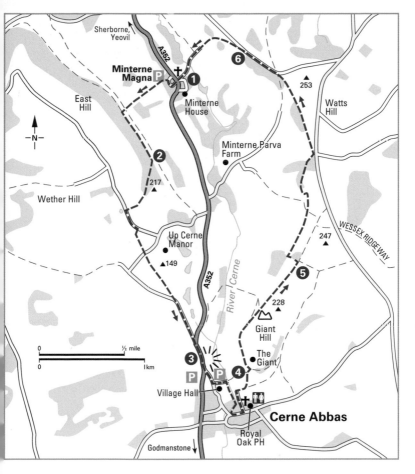

1. With the road behind you, take the bridleway up the left side of the car park, which soon bends right and then left round some trees, and left again. Keep right at a fork, to follow the track uphill. At the top, turn left on a broad grassy track inside the woods.

2. After 0.25 miles (400m) fork right, down through the woods. At the bottom turn left along the road. In 200yds (183m) take the footpath up right, signed 'Up Cerne'. Ignore the direction of the signpost (almost directly at Up Cerne Manor) and head up past the right-hand side of a line of trees then turn sharp left around them, aiming towards the right-hand of two white gates. Cross a road, pass to the right of this gate, and continue diagonally down the field, with Up Cerne Manor in view to the left. Pass to the right of a pond to rejoin the road. At its end bear right on the A352.

3. Soon cross to the car park for the best view of the Giant. Fork left on the road down to the village and turn left, signposted 'Village Hall'. Turn right beside the stream, signposted 'Village Centre'. Continue downstream to the High Street. On passing the back entrance to Abbots tearooms, ignore the footbridge to the left. Turn left, and left again in front of the New Inn, and left

by the Royal Oak, to pass the church. Walk past The Pitchmarket to the abbey. Turn right into the churchyard and bear left. Go through a gate and take the left-hand path to the base of Giant's Hill.

4. Cross a stile, then keep ahead up some steps. Now follow the path to the left, round the contour of the hill below the fence protecting the Cerne Giant. After another 0.25 miles (400m), the path slants uphill through thorny scrub. At the slope top, cross a stile by a fingerpost and slant left across a field to another fingerpost.

5. Here turn left, signed 'Wessex Ridgeway', and go down through a gate. Soon turn right through a galvanised gate and follow the bridleway path contouring around the hillside below fields. The path goes straight on through a gate inside the top edge of some woods to emerge at a gate near the road. Don't go through, but turn left away from the road (signed 'Minterne Magna'), through a field gate then along the left edge of a large field. At a gateway turn left on a gravel lane.

6. Directly above Minterne House, with a radio mast in sight ahead, turn left through a small gate signed 'Minterne Magna'. Slant gently downhill away from the fence, to the left of two redundant metal gateposts mid-field. Bear left down to a gate, then head directly downhill, following fingerposts. Join a track, which runs out to the left of the church to return to the car park.

Where to eat and drink
Cerne Abbas has three pubs, all with gardens, and Abbots serves meals and cream teas. The Minterne Gardens café is also open to the public, regardless of whether they visit the gardens.

What to see
Hidden from the main road behind high stone walls, Minterne House is a large Victorian pile. Its magnificent gardens are open to the public.

While you're there
Explore nearby Godmanstone where the now sadly closed Smiths Arms used to claim that it was the smallest pub in England. It is said that Charles II was passing and asked at the forge. The blacksmith said that he could not oblige as he had no licence, so the King granted him one.

HIGHER MELCOMBE AND THE BINGHAMS

DISTANCE/TIME	5 miles (8km) / 2hrs 30min
ASCENT/GRADIENT	443ft (135m) / ▲ ▲
PATHS	Farmland, woodland track, ancient bridleway, road
LANDSCAPE	Gently rolling farmland, little lumpy hills, village
SUGGESTED MAP	OS Explorer 117 Cerne Abbas & Bere Regis
START/FINISH	Grid reference: ST764031
DOG FRIENDLINESS	Some road walking, one unfriendly stile
PARKING	Small parking area on north side of village hall
PUBLIC TOILETS	None on route

Be prepared for confusion on this walk: it passes Higher Melcombe and then goes through Melcombe Bingham to Binghams Melcombe, which is also known as Melcombe Horsey. And Melcombe Horsey was the name of a village at Higher Melcombe that has now disappeared. Is that clear?

There has been a church at Binghams Melcombe since before 1302. The current one dates from the 14th century. The roving bell, 'Regina Coeli Alla Alla', was sold twice to raise funds for the church but kept coming back, eventually resting on the floor for 50 years until the money could be raised to rehang it. Today it's safely back with its companion 'O Beata Trinitas' in the belfry, although only chiming is allowed. The church is cruciform, with two side chapels forming the arms of the cross. The Bingham chapel has a touching memorial to Thomas, infant son of Richard and Philadelphia Bingham, who died in 1711. The Binghams were one of Dorset's leading parliamentary families during the Civil War, and their mansion and gardens (not open to the public), of which you can only catch a glimpse, are magnificent. The Dower House, opposite the church, has fine octagonal windowpanes.

Higher Melcombe is a solitary farm, set in a fertile green basin at the head of a valley. The buildings are dominated by the old manor house, built in the mid-15th century for Sir John Horsey, with a chapel attached later. A village called Melcombe Horsey once occupied this lovely spot. According to the map the village simply disappeared in medieval times, but why? Unlike Milton Abbas there is no sign of grand rebuilding. What could cause rural depopulation on such a scale? The answer lies at Dorset's other Melcombe, the port of Melcombe Regis, now absorbed into the sprawl of Weymouth. In June 1348, the first case in Britain of bubonic plague – the Black Death – was brought ashore here. The disease, carried by fleas that were equally at home on black rats and people, spread through the county with devastating speed, wiping out between a third and a half of the population.

The feudal system that had operated until this time in Dorset, in which labourers had been tied to manorial land, could not survive in the face of such losses. With a drastic shortage of able bodies, labour became a prime commodity. Workers simply moved to where they could be paid for their work as free men. Once-thriving villages such as Melcombe Horsey were reduced to little hamlets, or sometimes just a single, isolated farm. The changes meant a great reduction in arable cultivation, to the extent that some prime farmland reverted to more manageable grazing.

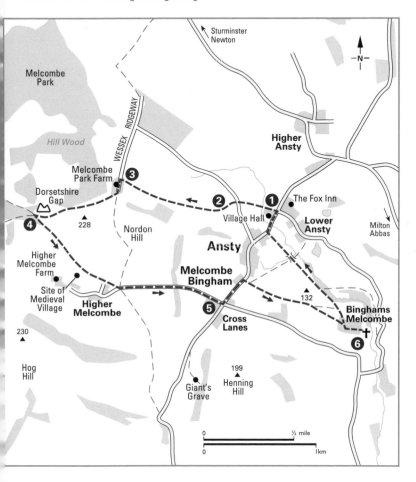

1. Leave the parking area and turn left up the road, then go immediately left over a stile and down a waymarked path. Cross a stile, bear down the right edge of the field and cross a stile at the bottom. Continue straight up the next field. Cross a stile and road to go through a gate. Keep straight on, aiming just to the right of an electricity pole in the hedge to reach a pair of stiles in that hedge.

2. Go over these stiles then bear diagonally across the field, in line with the farmhouse on the skyline, to leave by the far corner. Keep forward in the next field beside a hedge, then go through a gate at the top and go slightly right to the fingerpost and gate just to the right of the farmhouse.

3. Turn left, signed 'Dorset Gap', up through the farmyard and, just beyond, take the right-hand of three gates. Walk along the right edge of the field, above a wood. Go through a pair of gates and continue straight ahead along the top of the ridge, enjoying superb views over Blackmoor Vale. The track descends abruptly. Turn right, through a gate, to a crossroads of tracks at the Dorsetshire Gap.

4. Turn left along a bridleway through a deep cleft, signposted 'Higher Melcombe'. Keep left at another fingerpost at the edge of the wood. Go along a green lane and keep straight on the right edge of two fields. Ridges and hummocks in a field to your right are the only signs of the medieval village. Pass two farms at Higher Melcombe, at a junction of bridleways, and go through a gate and turn left, onto a minor road, or walk along the avenue that runs alongside (look right to see the hill track leading to the Giant's Grave). Descend past some houses to a junction.

5. Turn left and walk on the road into Melcombe Bingham. Pass a row of houses then turn right before the first thatched house, signposted 'Binghams Melcombe'. Go through a gateway to take the path across the field, bearing a little to the left, to join a fence. Maintain your direction, with the fence to your right, over a stile and through a strip of woodland. Continue ahead, across the centre of the field downhill towards Binghams Melcombe. Cross a stile and turn right. Follow the drive round and down to the church.

6. Retrace your route to the stile; do not cross it but continue up the grassy avenue. Before the end, turn left through a gate and go along a path in a copse. Bear left at each division of the path. Cross a stile and follow the right edge of the field, then bear right to go through a gateway and descend on a track. Go straight ahead to cross a gated footbridge. Keep straight on, bear right over a kissing gate in the fence and continue down the field. The path soon rises up a bank and goes through a gate, along a wooded strip and through another gate to reach the road. Turn right to return to your car.

Where to eat and drink
The Fox Inn at Ansty is a civilised pub with rooms. You can get morning coffee and snacks at the bar (dogs are welcome) or treat yourself to a meal in one of the two restaurants. Children are welcome throughout the pub.

What to see
Ansty's handsome, flint and brick village hall is called the Old Brewery Hall. It was the original brewery for Hall and Woodhouse beer, made since 1777. Hall and Woodhouse moved to Blandford St Mary in 1899 and still thrives there today under its better-known Badger trademark.

While you're there
What better explanation for a burial mound some 23ft (7m) long than that a giant lies entombed there? Take the footpath up the western slope of Henning Hill, to the south of Melcombe Bingham. On a terrace on the hillside you'll find the Giant's Grave. A so-called pillow mound lies near by, and there are good views along the valley.

MILTON ABBAS TO WINTERBORNE CLENSTON

DISTANCE/TIME	6.5 miles (10.4km) / 3hrs
ASCENT/GRADIENT	755ft (230m) / ▲ ▲
PATHS	Village High Street, easy forest roads, muddy bridleways, minor road, farm tracks
LANDSCAPE	Villages, mixed forest, rolling farmland with hidden valleys
SUGGESTED MAP	AA Walker's Map 6 Poole, Bournemouth & Purbeck
START/FINISH	Grid reference: ST806018
DOG FRIENDLINESS	Mostly good but some road walking
PARKING	On main street of Milton Abbas
PUBLIC TOILETS	None on route

Rarely do you find a village as symmetrical as Milton Abbas. It is the natural order of villages to grow over generations, to sprawl a little, develop secret corners and reflect different ages and tastes in their buildings. But in Milton Abbas you will find regular, whitewashed houses, identical in design, placed neatly on either side of a narrow defile. They face each other across the open street, thatched cowl facing thatched cowl. It's unnatural and slightly eerie. On closer inspection, you see that rebels have managed to sneak on a porch here, a coat of cream-coloured paint there, but nothing to seriously spoil the effect. No concessions were made to the two houses that were once the bakery and the forge, although the tailor's house had bow windows for extra light.

The explanation for this curiosity lies with the great house round the corner, the dream of Joseph and Caroline Damer, who bought Milton Abbey in 1752. It was on a fabulous site, first picked out by King Athelstan in AD 935, but the house left much to be desired. In 1771 the Damers decided to build something altogether grander, and more in keeping with their rising social status, to include a landscaped park by the most fashionable gardener of his day, Lancelot 'Capability' Brown. One thing was getting in their way, however: the untidy township that had grown up around the abbey was spoiling the view. It would have to go. Consequently a neat, new hamlet was built out of sight in a narrow valley, with a new church of pinkish stone. The houses look generous, but in fact each little block was two independent family dwellings, separated by a shared central hall. There were not enough new houses to go round, and overcrowding was a problem. The steep terraced gardens that were eventually dug out are one of the most attractive features of Milton Abbas today. The Damers are buried in splendour in the abbey church. Meanwhile, nearby Winterborne Clenston is altogether more organic. It has a Tudor manor house and a medieval tithe barn covered by a steep, chequerboard roof of alternating red and black squares. The Gothic-style Church of St Nicholas dates from 1840.

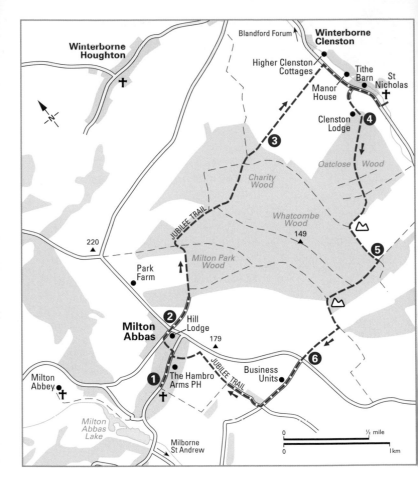

1. From the church take the road up the hill. Just after the Old Village Hall picnic area, take the second left turn (not the five-barred gate) through woodland. At the top keep right, into a residential road, and right again, to meet the road into the village by Hill Lodge.

2. Cross over and go down the private road, signposted as a bridleway. Follow this down and bend left, then right. Before a green metal gateway turn left up the steep path, signed as a bridleway and 'Jubilee Trail'. Descend to a track. Turn left and in a few paces, go up to the right. Bear right (signed 'bridleway') at the top, onto a track. Follow this track, ignoring forks to left and right, for about 1 mile (1.6km) to a crossroads in a dip. At the crossroads keep straight ahead. At a fork of waymarked bridleways bear right.

3. Emerge at a field to follow the path down, with Higher Clenston Cottages coming gradually into view. At the bottom turn right on a road through Winterborne Clenston, with its manor house, thatched barn, tiled tithe barn and Gothic Revival church. Turn left to visit the church. Retrace your steps to the thatched barn and turn left up the unsigned steep bridleway. This becomes an unmade track, passing below Clenston Lodge.

4. Bear left off the track near the top to pass beside a metal barrier, and follow the overgrown path, which bends to the right. Ignore minor forks and walk 0.5 miles (800m) through the woods, over two crossings of paths, the first of which appears to be a fork at first sight – go ahead here (the left option). After some time, the path narrows and bends right, to a field by a gate. Turn right to skirt the field inside the forest fence. At the bottom, turn left along a track.

5. At a junction turn right. After 0.5 miles (800m) and just as the track is about to curve up to the right look for a path on the left, and follow this to the field corner. Turn left up a steep path. Continue up the edge of the field, to swing right at the end to follow the hedge to the road.

6. Cross over and walk straight up the lane, passing Luccombe business units. Pass a pair of cottages and turn right through a gateway, up a track signed 'Jubilee Trail'. Where it almost meets the road at a fingerpost in trees to your right, bear diagonally left to go through a gate in the fence. Drop down to a second gate, and a clear path, signed 'Jubilee Trail', descends to emerge on the village street. Turn left to return to the start of the walk.

Where to eat and drink

The Hambro Arms is a long, low, thatched building on the High Street in Milton Abbas. In summer you can enjoy a scrumptious lunch outside on a bench at the front; in winter retreat indoors to the log burner to enjoy hearty fare, which includes bar food and daily specials with set meals on Sunday. Children are welcome in the dining area, and dogs in the bar area.

What to see

Brown tourist signs point the way to Milton Abbey, 0.5 miles (800m) up the valley. The house is now a school, but you can park amid the school buildings (donation box) and walk through to the abbey church. It was rebuilt in stone and flint after a disastrous fire of 1309 and has been restored several times since. Approach from the village of Hilton for the best views.

While you're there

Pay a visit to the nearby village of Winterborne Houghton to listen for owls. The inhabitants of this small community were once known as Houghton Owls after a tale in which one of their number, losing himself in the woods, called out for help. The cries of owls that he heard in response to his pleas he mistook for human voices. A strikingly similar episode occurs in Thomas Hardy's *Far from the Madding Crowd*, so it's quite possible that the great novelist appropriated the story.

GALLOWS CORNER AND MILTON ABBAS

DISTANCE/TIME	5 miles (8km) / 2hrs
ASCENT/GRADIENT	700ft (213m) / ▲ ▲ ▲
PATHS	Field paths and tracks, with short sections along lanes
LANDSCAPE	Steeply rolling farmland and woodland clumps
SUGGESTED MAP	AA Walker's Map 6 Poole, Bournemouth & Purbeck
START/FINISH	Grid reference: ST806018
DOG FRIENDLINESS	On leads along lanes and near grazing livestock
PARKING	Roadside parking in Milton Abbas
PUBLIC TOILETS	None on route

Æthelstan, regarded as the first English king, founded Milton Abbey in AD 933 as a memorial to his half-brother Edwin, who was drowned in a shipwreck. Æthelstan later received a vision predicting his victory over the Norse, and donated relics of St Sampson of Dol, on whose feast day the revelation occurred. The relics, together with the monastery, were completely destroyed by fire in 1309 after the wooden tower was struck by lightning. Although work began almost immediately on a new church, it was still ongoing by the time Henry VIII fell out with Rome and turned his attentions to relieving the monasteries of their wealth and power. The monks were evicted, and the abbey was bought by Sir John Tregonwell. Close to the King, he had, among other things, arranged the annulment of Henry's first marriage to Catherine of Aragon and overseen the closure of several monasteries, including Milton. Tregonwell allowed the church to remain in use for the parish but took the abbot's residence for his own house.

When Joseph Damer – later Baron Milford – acquired the estate in the middle of the 18th century, he demolished the old monastery, retaining only the great hall and the church as his private chapel. In its place he built a grand mansion and employed 'Capability' Brown to landscape the park and create a lake. The work involved demolishing the old village (which offended him on counts of both sight and smell) and banishing it, together with a new church, to the adjacent valley, today's Milton Abbas. Although the thatched cottages now look quite idyllic, at the time they were severely overcrowded, with each being intended to house two large families who had to use a common front door. The almshouses facing the church were re-sited from the old village, having been built there 100 years previously in 1674. In the middle of the 19th century, the merchant banker Carl Joachim Hambro bought the estate and set about restoring both the mansion and church, a commission he entrusted to Sir George Gilbert Scott. The Hambro family stayed there until 1932, after which the estate was broken up and the mansion eventually bought for the establishment of Milton Abbey School in 1954.

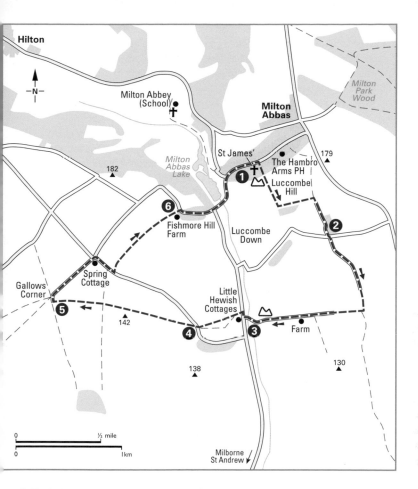

1. Begin in the centre of the village by St James' Church, going up a footpath signed 'Luccombe Hill' to the left of the churchyard. This climbs steeply through the wood behind the church, mainly by steps. At the top, continue through gates up a grass bank onto the edge of a field and head straight across over the rise of Luccombe Hill to the corner of a wood, which soon appears at the far side. Turn left beside the trees to the corner of the field, then swing right though a gap along a hedged bridleway signed to the A354.

2. Emerging onto a lane, go left and immediately right onto another track. Later losing the left hedge, carry on at the field edge and leave through a kissing gate in the corner. Walk on by the left hedge to another kissing gate. Through that, turn right and climb away at the edge of a couple of fields. Keep ahead over the crest past a farm and follow its track out to a lane at the bottom of the hill.

3. Go right past Little Hewish Cottages, leaving some 20yds (18m) beyond along a bridle track signed left through a gate. Climb to a second gate and continue over the shoulder of the hill beside a sparse hedge on your left. Keep ahead at the far end to exit through a gate onto another lane.

4. Cross to a path opposite. Bear half right to climb across the field to the top corner. Pass through a wooded gap and continue at the right edge of two more fields over the top of the hill. Leave through a gate in the corner into a wooded strip that conceals a crossing track. Turn right to a junction at Gallows Corner.

5. Signed to Milton Abbas, the track to the right tunnels downhill to emerge at a junction of lanes by Spring Cottage. Walk right towards Milborne St Andrew. After 300yds (274m), just before a farmhouse, turn back sharp left on an unmarked rising track. Through a gate into fields at the top, continue over the crest of the hill. Pass through the right-hand one of two adjacent gates and carry on at the edge of successive fields, going through a gate onto a grassy track and dropping out at the bottom through Fishmore Hill farmyard onto a lane.

6. Follow it steeply downhill to a junction beside a lodge at the entrance to Milton Abbas Lake. Take the lane ahead, from which there is a glimpse through the trees on the left to the lake. Keep right at the next junction back into Milton Abbas.

Where to eat and drink
The Hambro Arms sits at the top of the village – a long, thatched building that perfectly blends with its surroundings. It is open all day for breakfast, lunch, afternoon tea and dinner, serving food at the bar and full meals in the library restaurant. There's a selection of real ales at the bar and an extensive wine menu to accompany the food.

What to see
Gruesomely named, Gallows Corner describes exactly what it was, the site of a gibbet, where wrongdoers were often left hanging as a dire warning to others. In those days, punishment was harsh and the ultimate penalty wasn't just reserved for murder; sheep stealing and even petty theft could result in a stretched neck.

While you're there
Although the school is obviously private there is a footpath through the grounds and the church is open to visitors. Inside is a white marble funerary monument by the Italian sculptor Carlini to Caroline, the wife of Joseph Damer, and the tombs of John and Mary Tregonwell, as well as a striking Tree of Jesse window by Augustus Pugin. Outside is a sign describing how the young John Tregonwell fell from the abbey roof when only 5 years old, landing completely unhurt after his pantaloons billowed into a parachute.

BADBURY RINGS AND SHAPWICK

DISTANCE/TIME	7.5 miles (12.1km) / 3hrs 30min
ASCENT/GRADIENT	459ft (140m) / ▲
PATHS	Farm tracks, roads, grassy lanes and fields
LANDSCAPE	Gently rolling farmland leading down to water-meadows
SUGGESTED MAP	AA Walker's Map 6 Poole, Bournemouth & Purbeck
START/FINISH	Grid reference: ST959031
DOG FRIENDLINESS	Under control on Badbury Rings, but this is under review; some road walking
PARKING	Car park (donation) at Badbury Rings, signposted off B3082 from Wimborne to Blandford
PUBLIC TOILETS	None on route

The most obvious legacy of the Roman invasion of Britain in AD 43 is the network of straight military roads. Before they came, many routes existed as tracks, but it took the Roman desire for effective communication and control across their empire to make these permanent. A few roads would actually have been paved, but usually fine gravel was layered over coarser chippings for effective drainage (a forerunner of modern tarmac).

Four of the most important Roman routes across Dorset met at the hub of Badbury Rings. The most famous and visible of these is Ackling Dyke, the major road which linked London (Londinium) with Old Sarum (Sorviodunum), Dorchester (Durnovaria) and Exeter (Iscarduniorum). Badbury Rings was a massive fort, occupying a spectacular vantage point. Bronze Age barrows confirm a settlement here around 2000 BC, and the fort dates from the sixth century BC. At that time Dorset was inhabited by the Durotriges tribe, prosperous Iron Age traders, farmers and potters. The indications are that the Second Augusta Legion, under the command of Vespasian (who would later become emperor) had built an advance base at Lake Farm, beside the River Stour at Wimborne. They realised the strategic importance of Badbury and attacked and took control of the hilltop. The fort was dismantled, and the inhabitants killed, sold into slavery or otherwise dispersed. The Romans went on to build their own fortified citadel called Vindocladia, nearby at Shapwick.

When the Romans finally withdrew from Britain in the fifth century, this site was absorbed back into the Dorset landscape, like so many other Roman structures. Badbury Rings did not disappear from history, however. Many believe that it was the site of Mount Badon, where King Arthur won a legendary battle against the Saxons around AD 516. In 1645 the fort served as a meeting place for the Dorset Clubmen, a ragged, badly armed force opposing both parties in the Civil War. Over 4,000 gathered to hear speeches by local notables. They were subsequently routed by Cromwell's New Model Army.

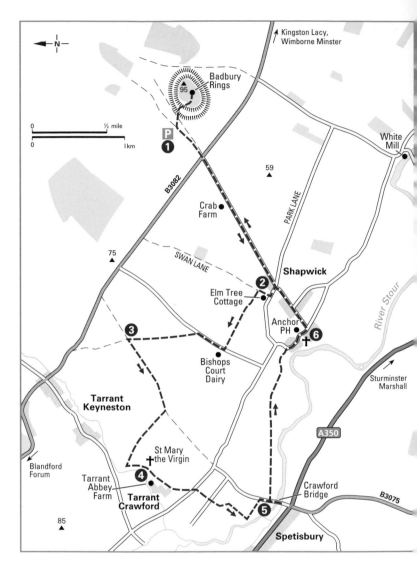

1. Walk up the hill to explore the site of Badbury Rings, then head down the track by which you drove in. Cross the B3082 and go straight down the road towards Shapwick – its straightness gives away its Roman origins. Pass Crab Farm on your right, with winter views of Charborough Tower on the distant horizon.

2. At the junction with Park Lane turn right, then right again by Elm Tree Cottage to go up Swan Lane, a grassy track. Turn left over a stile before the gate. Go straight over the field, cross a stile, and along the left edge of the next field. Go into the yard of Bishops Court Dairy and turn right past the first barn. Go up a track and bear left at a track through a gateway, then half right across the field, heading for a narrow gap halfway along the hedge. Go through this and continue in the same direction to the top corner of the field.

3. Cross a stile and turn left down the broad bridleway. After 980yds (800m) pass a line of trees. Turn right, up a track between high hedges (following the blue public bridleway marker) which levels off and begins to drop. Continue walking with glimpses of Tarrant Crawford church blending into trees on your left. Follow the track round to the left, by the side of a stream.

4. Go through a gate and reach the church on your left. Continue towards the barns of Tarrant Abbey Farm. Just before a field gate pointedly wrapped in barbed wire, go left through a bridle gate and continue diagonally across the field to a track between fences. Follow this uphill, passing above the farmhouse. At the top of the track go through a gate and head straight over the next field. Cross the road and walk down the right edge of the field. Go through a gate and cross another road into a green lane. Bear left through a gate and then diagonally right across a field to a gate in the far corner. Go through this gate onto the road and turn right.

5. Walk onto the old Crawford Bridge, just to admire it. Retrace your steps and turn right at the footpath sign. Cross a stile and walk straight across the meadows for a mile (1.6km). When you reach a fence on the left, walk round it to a gate. Go through and follow the track round to the right. Keep right at a fork where a left turn leads into a field. Cross a stile behind the farm and walk along a farm track then bear right along the road into the village.

6. Pass the Anchor pub and turn left, passing Piccadilly Lane on your right-hand side. Go straight up the road, now retracing your route back to the car park at Badbury Rings.

Where to eat and drink
The red-brick Anchor free house in the centre of Shapwick goes out of its way to welcome families (dogs are welcome at the bar end). The menu includes many ingredients sourced locally. Try braised shoulder of lamb or the slow-roast pork belly. There's also a good vegetarian choice, and vegan selections too.

What to see
Don't miss the isolated little grey Abbey Church of St Mary the Virgin in Tarrant Crawford. Once a nunnery, its simple interior has dark wood pews, panelling around the altar and a Jacobean pulpit. Some details of its 14th-century wall painting of the legend of St Margaret of Antioch are still discernible.

While you're there
In an idyllic setting beside the River Stour at Sturminster Marshall is White Mill, a beautifully restored corn mill. Just to the west of Wimborne you'll find Kingston Lacy, a delightful mansion set in vast parkland. Built in 1663 for the Bankes family after the destruction Corfe Castle, today the house has a fine collection of paintings. Both the mill and the house are preserved by the National Trust.

WIMBORNE MINSTER AND ITS WATER-MEADOWS

DISTANCE/TIME	4 miles (6.4km) / 2hrs
ASCENT/GRADIENT	Negligible
PATHS	Riverside path (may be muddy), pavement, field paths, lane, gates
LANDSCAPE	Town centre and water-meadows to southwest
SUGGESTED MAP	AA Walker's Map 6 Poole, Bournemouth & Purbeck
START/FINISH	Grid reference: ST995001
DOG FRIENDLINESS	Town walking on very narrow pavements close to traffic makes this walk less dog-friendly
PARKING	Gravel car park on Cowgrove Road (unsigned) beyond football ground
PUBLIC TOILETS	Near Minster church

Wimborne is surrounded by the picturesque, gentle folds of the Dorset countryside, yet is just 5 miles (8km) from seaside towns such as Poole. The town grew up at the confluence of two rivers: the River Stour and the River Allen, both excellent for fishing. This attractive market town has retained many of its historic buildings, some dating to the 15th century. The High Street, in particular, boasts most of its original buildings, although they now house a variety of 21st-century retailers, coffee shops and restaurants. A bustling place year-round, Wimborne attracts many tourists, especially at weekends and during summer when, above the noise of the through-traffic and the busy shoppers, the town crier can be heard ringing his bell and yelling out information and announcements about the place.

Dominating the skyline and the narrow streets of the town is Wimborne Minster. The building's foundation dates to AD 705, when Cuthberga and Cwenburga, sisters to Ina, King of the West Saxons, set up a mixed monastery here. Some 500 nuns were trained, and many nuns went from here with St Boniface to spread their teachings to pagan tribes in Germany. Cuthberga died in AD 725 and was buried in a Saxon church, thought to be on the same ground as the Minster. And, in AD 871, Alfred the Great's brother, King Ethelred, was buried here after being killed in a battle in the area against the Danes. At the beginning of the 11th century, part of the minster was destroyed for good, and the present and remaining church building was constructed by the Normans with some Gothic parts. In 1600, the 13th-century spire, which was above the minster's smaller tower, came crashing through the church, but miraculously no one was killed. One of the minster's most fascinating features is the library, founded for the free use of the townspeople in 1686, and consisting of 350 (mainly theological) volumes. To prevent theft, the books were chained to the shelves. Also interesting are the two leather fire buckets in the baptistry – all that remains of the minster's 18th-century fire equipment.

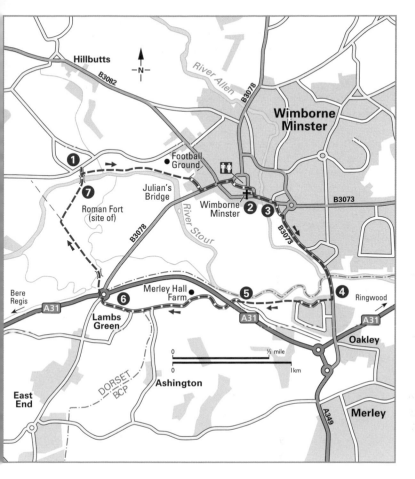

1. Turn left through a wide gate and into a field. Follow the path beside the river for 0.5 miles (800m), on the Stour Valley Way, crossing two stiles and a very short footbridge before reaching the football ground, up to your left. This gives way to allotments. The mottled brown towers of the minster are now seen ahead. The allotment track runs into a little side road. Turn left at the end, towards the town centre, passing through a residential area of Victorian villas and modern houses – this is Julian's Road. Emerge opposite the Minster Arms and cross straight over into West Street. Continue along the narrow pavement round past the back of the King's Head Hotel into the town's main square. Turn right here, into Church Street, passing the Oddfellows Arms pub and then the toilets on the left, with the minster straight ahead.

2. Take some time to visit the minster; its squat, square towers dominate the town centre. The present building dates from around 1100. After exploring the minster walk past the No.9 On the Green café on the left, to meet the High Street. Follow this round to the right, to the junction with King Street and East Street. Turn left here, with a glimpse of the stream on your left. Pass the Rising Sun pub on your right, cross the river and keep straight on.

3. Shortly afterwards, bear right down Poole Road and continue on to pass a large thatched pub, the Coach and Horses, on the left. Cross the River Stour on a footbridge to one side of the old arched road bridge.

4. Almost immediately turn right, down a narrow path between houses, sign-posted 'Stour Valley Way - Corfe Mullen'. This emerges on to a bungalow estate; go straight over a mini-roundabout and follow the aquamarine way-markers through the estate. Next, after about 55yds (50m), bear right down a narrow footpath, sided by fences, across the bottom of a recreation ground. Go through a metal kissing gate to continue on along a line of trees (on your right), above a bend of the river. There are water-meadows below – look out for cormorants in the river. Cross a stile and turn up left, along the edge of some woods (on your right).

5. Go through a kissing gate and emerge at a lane and turn right (it's noisy from the bypass, which runs parallel). Zig-zag under the bypass and go up to a gate. Go through and along the road, past Merley Hall farmhouse on your right. Continue ahead and at the end of the lane cross over the road immediately and turn right to reach a very busy roundabout (A31).

6. Follow the path round to the left and cross straight over this road with care. Once across, look directly ahead for the wooden fingerpost located in the bushes, signposted 'Stour Valley Way and Pamphill'. Cross the stile and follow a grassy track as it bends to the right. Cross another stile over a fence, staying on the broad green track. Bear left to go through a metal gate, then cross a footbridge and go through another metal gate, before bearing right on a path over the grass. Keep right at a mid-field fork to pass through an old hedge-line and soon turn right, to cross a stile in the fence. Head straight across the meadows towards the river. Meet the corner of another field but continue straight ahead in the same field, close to its right-hand hedge and fence.

7. Go through a metal kissing gate. Cross a high footbridge over the river. On the opposite bank a surfaced riverside path leads off to the left. Bear right on this path to return to the car park, passing a slipway for launching small craft.

Where to eat and drink
The Oddfellows Arms, commended for its garden, offers morning coffee, as well as home-cooked bar food. The Rising Sun has a riverside garden and terrace, and offers a selection of sandwiches, jacket potatoes and a children's menu. The No.9 On the Green café overlooks the minster and is housed in a building that dates from 1590.

What to see
The Stour supports a rich variety of wildlife. Most obvious are the birds, but look too for fish and butterflies.

While you're there
Visit the Priest's House Museum on the High Street, a medieval house with later additions. It's full of the domestic paraphernalia of years gone by, including a Victorian kitchen and a tinsmith's workshop.

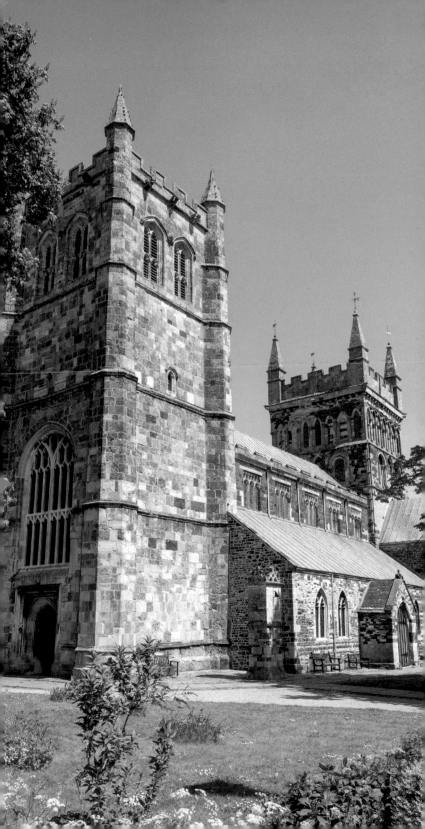

TOLPUDDLE AND AROUND

DISTANCE/TIME	4.5 miles (7.2km) / 2hrs 30min
ASCENT/GRADIENT	394ft (120m) / ▲
PATHS	Farm tracks, field paths, pathless field edges
LANDSCAPE	Gently rolling farmland above the valley of the River Piddle
SUGGESTED MAP	AA Walker's Map 6 Poole, Bournemouth & Purbeck
START/FINISH	Grid reference: SY787945
DOG FRIENDLINESS	Some road walking
PARKING	Lay-by beside Martyrs Museum; or High Street
PUBLIC TOILETS	None on route

The sleepy Dorset village of Tolpuddle, astride the Puddle (or Piddle) river, entered the history books in 1834 when six of its farm labourers became what would later become known as the Tolpuddle Martyrs. Trade unions had become technically legal a few years before and, faced with a pay cut to six shillings a week – the rough equivalent of £30 at today's prices – the six had formed themselves into the Friendly Society of Agricultural Labourers. Under Tolpuddle's sycamore tree, the six swore an oath of solidarity and secrecy. It was this that led to their conviction at Dorchester Assizes on a spurious charge of 'administering unlawful oaths'.

The Tolpuddle six joined the 165,000 men, women and children shipped out as convicts to Australia between the 'First Fleet' of 1786 and 1850. Of these, about 1,800 individuals had been convicted of political crimes. They included Luddites and rioters, Chartists and radicals. These 'dangerous elements' were effectively silenced by being sent to another, apparently godforsaken, world. In defence of the Martyrs, the infant trade-union movement organised one of the first-ever protest marches, and 800,000 people of all classes signed a petition for their release. Under the new Whig government of 1830 their sentences were quashed. Even so, it took five years to bring them all home. The Martyrs had developed a taste for life beyond these little valleys, however, and after returning to Dorset five of them emigrated again, to Ontario in Canada. The only one to live out his life in the village was James Hammett; his grave is seen in the village churchyard. Today, the TUC runs an annual Martyrs Festival with speeches, music and a parade, in the third week in July.

Outside the Martyrs Museum is a statue of one of the men, George Loveless. He was an eloquent Methodist lay preacher, and on sentencing wrote the Martyrs' freedom song, still sung today: *God is our guide!/ From field, from wave,/ From plough, from anvil, and from loom;/ We come, our country's rights to save,/ And speak a tyrant faction's doom:/ We raise the watch-word liberty;/ We will, we will, we will be free!*

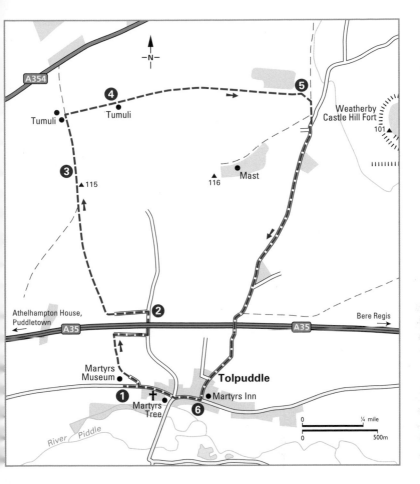

1. From the Martyrs Museum head towards the centre of the village. After about 110yds (100m), having passed a row of houses, turn up left, on a lane which hooks back behind the same houses. Continue up a path through scrubby woodland, towards the bypass. The path detours to cross this. So, at the top turn right along the tarmac track beside the bypass, then turn left through the underpass.

2. Turn left on another tarmac track, and continue to its end. Turn right through a hole in the hedge, and cross a large field diagonally uphill (roughly northwest) to a hedge gap. Head uphill (north) to left of a hedge, continuing along a second field over the hill brow and gently downhill. The comforting folds of Burleston Down are to your left.

3. Before the corner of the field bear right, to continue down a narrow path between high banks and trees. As the path levels out, at a post with blue markers, turn right through a gap in the hedge. Keep straight on (east) along the bottom of a gentle chalkland valley, following the hedge on your left. Look out for deer on the big sweep of chalk downland up to your right.

4. Pass some ruined barns on your left. At the corner of the second field bear left to a gate on the right, onto a visible tractor track. Go through a gate beside a collapsed corrugated shed and follow the valley floor, with scrubby woodland on your left.

5. At a broad double gateway (with a small gateway to the left) under beeches, with Weatherby Castle hill-fort almost blocking the valley ahead, turn right to join a tractor track running uphill beside a low-voltage power line. Where the track bends right into a field, keep ahead, to the left of the hedge, up to a gate into a green lane. At its top, continue ahead, to left of a hedge, over the crest of the hill, to the start of a well-used farm track. It leads down past a farm, to become a tarmac lane over the bypass and down to Tolpuddle, beside the Martyrs Inn.

6. Turn right and walk back towards the museum, passing the Martyrs Tree on the triangular green. Cross the street to enter the churchyard, and walk past the church to visit martyr James Hammett's grave. Leave the churchyard via a little wooden gate ahead and continue along the High Street to your car.

Where to eat and drink

Tolpuddle's friendly Martyrs Inn is open all day and serves a tasty range of pub food from lunchtime, including locally sourced meat and fresh fish. Children are welcome in the pub and restaurant, dogs and muddy-booted walkers in the public bar area.

What to see

The Martyrs Tree, a sycamore in the heart of Tolpuddle, is the source of the village's fame. It was a meeting point for the Friendly Society of Agricultural Labourers, formed to peaceably press their masters for better pay. At that time a local labourer's wage was just 7 shillings a week – around 3 shillings below what was paid elsewhere in Dorset. The six, picked out as trouble-makers, were George and James Loveless, Thomas and John Standfield, James Brine and James Hammett.

While you're there

Just down the road is Athelhampton, one of England's most majestic old mansions. Parts of it date from 1485. The house is stuffed with treasures, from Tudor architecture in the Great Hall to a carved Charles I tester bed. Allow time to explore the world-famous gardens with their yew topiary and fountains.

AROUND BOCKHAMPTON IN HARDY COUNTRY

DISTANCE/TIME	5 miles (8km) / 2hrs
ASCENT/GRADIENT	328ft (100m) / ▲ ▲
PATHS	Woodland and heathland tracks, muddy field paths and bridleways, firm paths, road
LANDSCAPE	Woodland, tree-clad heath, open meadows, waterway, rolling farmland
SUGGESTED MAP	AA Walker's Map 5 Weymouth & South Dorset
START/FINISH	Grid reference: SY725921
DOG FRIENDLINESS	Allowed in Hardy's garden but not cottage; deer shooting year-round in woods – keep dogs close
PARKING	National Trust's Thorncombe Wood (pay and display) by Visitor Centre
PUBLIC TOILETS	None on route; nearest northwest on A35

You can't go far in Dorset without coming across novelist and poet Thomas Hardy (1840–1928). He did more than anybody to establish an identity for the county, thinly disguised as a fictional Wessex. His complicated tales of thwarted desire and human failing, littered with memorable, realistic characters and evocative descriptions of recognisable places, and mostly with miserable endings, have become literary classics. Hardy was born at Higher Bockhampton in the cottage built by his great-grandfather, set in a lovely garden. The cottage is now owned by the National Trust.

In 1867 Hardy retired to Dorset for health reasons and began writing seriously. His first real success, *Far From the Madding Crowd* (1874), remains popular, helped by the classic 1967 film starring Julie Christie. After the success of this book he married Emma Gifford; they lived for a time at Sturminster Newton. It's *The Return of the Native* (1878) that memorably features 'Egdon Heath', the Dorset wildlands and almost a character in their own right. Already fragmented in Hardy's day, 'Egdon' now survives as the tiny patch southeast of his cottage crossed on this walk. Studland Heath also conveys the atmosphere described by Hardy: 'the mummied heathbells of the past summer, originally tender and purple, now washed colourless by Michaelmas rains, and dried to dead skins by October suns'.

In 1885 Hardy and his wife moved to the home he had designed at Max Gate, on the outskirts of Dorchester (his Casterbridge), and he remained there for the rest of his life. He was buried in Westminster Abbey. His heart, however, lies in Stinsford (his Mellstock) churchyard, between the tombs of his first and second wives, Emma Gifford and Florence Dugdale. The Hardy influence is still strong in Dorset. Fact and fiction become blurred in 'Tess's Cottage' and 'Casterbridge Agricultural College', and pubs proudly identify themselves as their fictional counterpart. A long-distance footpath, the Hardy Way, links many of the author's favourite sites.

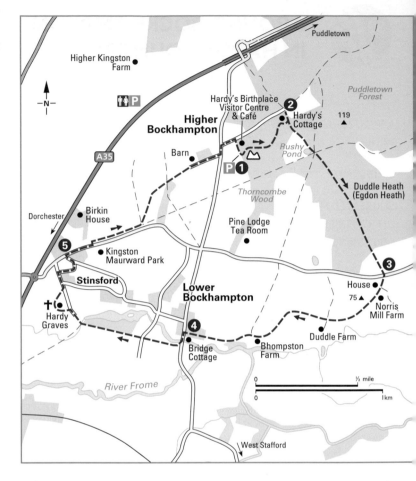

1. Take the steep woodland path to the right of the display boards, signposted 'Thorncombe Wood'. Turn left then right at signs for Hardy's Cottage, and follow the winding route down to a crossroads of tracks, marked by a monument. Turn left to visit Hardy's Cottage.

2. Retrace your route up behind the cottage and bear left, signed 'Rushy Pond', then immediately turn right on a path that bends right. At a crossroads by the pond take the path ahead signed 'Duddle Heath'. In 20yds (18m), at another crossroads, go straight across ('Norris Mill'); the path heads down to cross Hardy's 'Egdon Heath'. It crosses a track then goes through a gate to run under pines, with occasional yellow markers on trees. Go left at a fork and cross a stile, then turn sharp right (away from the nearby track) through trees to another stile. Bear left across a field to a stile and gate onto a road.

3. Cross the road into a farm track which keeps to the right of some barns. Where the track ends, cross a stile and bear right over a field. Cross a pair of stiles in the hedge, then go straight across the field to a stile and head across the driveway of Duddle Farm (left) and over another stile. Go ahead to cross a bridge and stiles down into a field. Follow its left edge to another stile, and

bear left, following a faint path round the base of the hill. Pass to the right of a brick house and walk up its drive through Bhompston Farm. Where the main track bends up to the right, take the track ahead through a wide pair of metal gates. After a few paces, bear left over a stile and walk along the field foot (signed 'Lwr Bock'ton'), with the River Frome nearby on the left. Cross a stile to reach a kissing gate. Cross the next field slightly uphill to a kissing gate to the right of farm buildings. Go through a field gate and the farmyard to its exit driveway to meet a road beside Bridge Cottage.

4. Turn left across the river and immediately turn right, on a riverside path which becomes a causeway. Ignore a first bridleway to the right, but just after the path crosses the river, turn right, signed 'Stinsford'. Bear left through a wooden gate into the churchyard, passing to the right of the church, with the Hardy graves to your right, as well as that of another great poet, Cecil Day-Lewis. Leave by the top gate and walk up the road past the Agricultural Academy. Turn right into a 20mph lane, then turn left to a lodge on the public road.

5. Turn right, up the road. After the entrance to Birkin House, bear left onto a good path and continue through woodland, alongside the road. After two gates, turn away from the road on a farm track, signposted 'Higher Bockhampton'. From here you can follow signs for Hardy's Birthplace Visitor Centre. Inside the field turn half right, slanting up a field, with woodland over on your right. At the field's top corner keep going straight on with the fence on your left until you come to a big shed. Here a green lane runs ahead to the road. Turn left, then right by the postbox, and right again to return to the car park.

Where to eat and drink

At the Visitor Centre by the car park you'll find the modern building housing the Under the Greenwood Tree Café. It's open daily and serves breakfast, lunches and cream teas. Just 0.5 miles (800m) east of waypoint 3, Pine Lodge Farm Tea Room, open Wednesday to Sunday, serves cream teas and lunches, and roasts on Sunday. Dogs are welcome at the outside seating area.

What to see

As you turn up from the watercourse towards Stinsford church, look left for the unusual sight of pictorial thatch. Though now obscured by the years, what looks like a bear and other animals have been carved into the thatched roofs of a cottage and its garage.

While you're there

Visit the formal Edwardian gardens and extensive parkland of Kingston Maurward. They include a rose garden, a Japanese garden, an outstanding double herbaceous border and an unusual red garden. The Georgian house is now occupied by an agricultural college. There's also a lively farm animal park and a visitor centre.

A CLIMB UP GOLDEN CAP

33

DISTANCE/TIME	4 miles (6.4km) / 2hrs 30min
ASCENT/GRADIENT	1,007ft (307m) / ▲ ▲ ▲
PATHS	Field tracks, country lanes, steep zig-zag gravel path
LANDSCAPE	Windswept coastline of lumps and bumps
SUGGESTED MAP	AA Walker's Map 11 Lyme Bay
START/FINISH	Grid reference: SY420917
DOG FRIENDLINESS	Some road walking; all the stiles have dog gates
PARKING	Car park (charge) above gravel beach in Seatown; beware, can flood in stormy weather
PUBLIC TOILETS	At end of road, Seatown

Golden Cap is the rather obvious name for a high, flat-topped hill of deep orange sandstone on the cliffs between Charmouth and Bridport. It represents the tail-end of a vein of warm-coloured sandstone. The Cap is the highest point on the south coast, at 627ft (191m), with views along the shore to the tip of Portland Bill in one direction and to Start Point in the other. Inland, you can see Pilsdon Pen.

Climbing towards the top of Golden Cap, you pass from neat fields, through a line of wind-scoured oak trees, into an area of high heathland, walking up through bracken, heather, bilberry and blackberry, alive with songbirds. The loose undercliff on the seaward side creates a different habitat. In botanical and wildlife terms, Golden Cap is one of the richest properties in the National Trust's portfolio. Today people associate the National Trust with grand houses, but its first acquisition, in 1896, was a stretch of coast in Wales.

On the very top of Golden Cap itself is a simple memorial to the Earl of Antrim, chairman of the National Trust in the 1960s and 1970s. It was he who spearheaded the National Trust's 1965 appeal campaign, named 'Enterprise Neptune', to purchase sections of unspoiled coastline before the developers could have a chance to move in. Golden Cap was part of this ambitious campaign, and over the years the National Trust has continued to buy up pockets of land all around this area, with the aim of preserving the traditional field pattern that exists in the region between Eype and Lyme Regis. The Trust's acquisition includes the ruined Chapel of St Gabriel's (which is now little more than a low shell with a porch to one side) and the neighbouring row of thatched cottages that have been smartly refurbished to a high standard and are now let out as visitor accommodation. They are all that now remains of the small fishing village of Stanton St Gabriel, sheltering in the valley behind the cliffs, which was largely abandoned after the coast road was rerouted inland in 1824; the chapel had fallen derelict long before this, however.

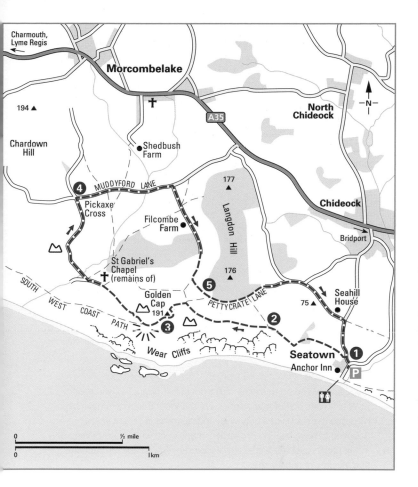

1. Walk back up through Seatown to the village edge. A gap on the left is signposted 'Golden Cap'. The path goes through a gate at the end, and crosses the field to a gate and footbridge into woodland. After two gates at the other side, bear right up the hill, signposted 'Golden Cap'.

2. Where the path forks by a bench keep left. Go through some trees and through a kissing gate. Bear left, around the open hillside, with Golden Cap ahead of you. Pass through a line of trees and walk up the fence. Go up some steps, through a gate, and continue ahead. At the fingerpost go left through a kissing gate to follow the path of shallow steps up through bracken, heather, bilberry and bramble to the top of Golden Cap.

3. Pass the trig point and carry on along the top to the left of a little stone coast path marker. After the stone memorial to the Earl of Antrim the path bends right and zig-zags steeply downhill, enjoying great views along the bay to Charmouth and Lyme Regis. Go through a gate and bear right over the field towards the ruined St Gabriel's Chapel. In the bottom corner turn down left through a gateway, passing the ruins on your right, then go through a gate. Go down the track, passing St Gabriel's manor house on

your left, and bear right down the farm road, signed 'Chardown Hill'. Follow this uphill between high banks and hedges, to Pickaxe Cross junction at the top of a tarmac lane. (Here you'd go straight on for St Wite's Well and Hardown Hill.)

4. Turn right, signed 'Langdon Hill', down the tarmac Muddyford Lane. Pass the gate of Shedbush Farm and continue uphill. Turn right up a concreted lane to Filcombe Farm. Bear left just beyond the farm buildings, following blue markers through two gates. Walk up the track, to go along the foot of the first field and straight across the next one. Head up left, ignoring the grassy track leading straight on and go over the green saddle between Langdon Hill and Golden Cap.

5. Go left through a gate in the corner and down a path (Pettycrate Lane) beside the woods, with sea views to the right. Ignore a footpath over a stile to the right. At a junction of tracks keep right, downhill. Pass Seahill House on your left and at the road turn right. Continue down into Seatown village to return to your car.

Where to eat and drink

The Anchor Inn at Seatown offers an interesting selection of ales, food and wine. The terrace overlooking the beach fills up quickly in summer. The rusted anchor outside belonged to the *Hope*, wrecked on Chesil Beach during a storm in 1748.

What to see

If you are extending this walk to Hardown Hill (Walk 34), you pass St Wite's Well, one of many springs in the West Country to have been raised to the status of a holy well, and restored in recent years. Believed to have healing properties, many such wells have origins in the pagan past but were later adopted by Christians for baptisms and as sites of pilgrimage.

While you're there

Moore's biscuit bakery in Morcombelake is a fascinating detour, worth it for the smell alone. Through a glass screen see the biscuits being made by hand – and sample as you watch. There's also a gallery of artwork associated with Moore's packaging. The famous savoury Dorset knobs, thrice-baked and explosively crisp, are a post-Christmas speciality. Open weekdays (and weekends in summer).

AROUND HARDOWN HILL

DISTANCE/TIME	5 miles (8km) / 2hrs
ASCENT/GRADIENT	760ft (232m) / ▲ ▲ ▲
PATHS	Mainly tracks and lanes
LANDSCAPE	Steeply rolling coastal downs
SUGGESTED MAP	AA Walker's Map 11 Lyme Bay
START/FINISH	Grid reference: SY383933
DOG FRIENDLINESS	On leads along lanes, near grazing livestock and at Upcot Farm
PARKING	Stonebarrow Hill (National Trust) car park, accessed via steep, narrow lane from eastern end of Charmouth
PUBLIC TOILETS	By National Trust shop at lower end of parking

A complex geology, undercut by the sea and lubricated by rainfall seeping through the strata, makes the Jurassic coast either side of Charmouth among the most unstable in England. The area known as Cain's Folly below Stonebarrow Hill is one of the largest ongoing landslides in the country, and large sections of cliff periodically slump towards the sea. A major slip in 1942 took out a wartime radar station, with subsequent slip events moving the safe line of the coast path ever inland.

This walk begins from the National Trust information centre on Stonebarrow Hill, housed in a 1950s radar station built in response to the increasing tensions of the Cold War. It follows a rising track that was once the road between Charmouth and Morcombelake, with today's route taking an easier line along the side of the Char valley. Morcombelake is clustered around Hardown Hill, a prominence whose summit gives 'one of the top twelve Dorset views that take your breath away' according to the county's official tourist website. Like many of Dorset's hills, it was used as a burial site during the Bronze Age. Among the items unearthed were spearheads, a shield boss, brooches and a knife, artefacts of an early Saxon warrior class.

Capping the hill are beds of greensand, which contain chert, a hard rock akin to flint. Hardown has been quarried since the medieval period, and the overgrown remains of pits and mine adits are scattered around the top. The lumps of chert, called 'cobs', were split into building stones using a long-handled hammer, with the cob being held in an iron claw and wrapped in wet sacking to prevent flying splinters.

The hilltop heath is composed mainly of ling and gorse, but includes other heathers and bilberry. Common dodder is prevalent, a vine-like parasitic plant that attaches to the roots of heather and gorse. It appears as a tangle of ruddy-brown stems entwined around its host, producing clusters of tiny pale pink flowers. Lower down you will find heath bedstraw, Devil's bit scabious, wood sage and masses of bluebell. The hedgerows lining the old tracks can be thick with red campion, foxgloves, herb Robert and vetch. In early summer the flower meadows on Chardown Hill and Stonebarrow attract hundreds of butterflies such as the common blue, pearl-bordered fritillary and marbled white. Among the flowers is the peculiarly named corky-fruited water dropwort, which can grow up to 3ft (1m) high and produces dense pink-tinged flowers. Wildlife to watch for includes the stonechat, whose name describes a song that sounds like two pebbles being knocked together. Kestrels and buzzards patrol the skies, while up on the heath on warm days you could come across an adder or common lizard taking advantage of the sun. At dusk you might spot the rare lesser horeshoe bat, which roosts in the old mine adits.

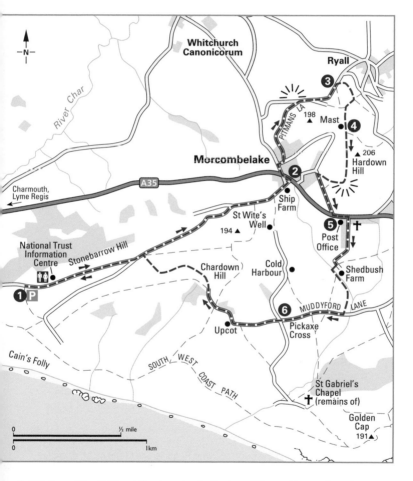

1. Climb past the National Trust centre to the top of the parking and continue through a gate at the end along a hedged track towards Chardown Hill and Morcombelake. Beyond the crest, the track gradually falls towards the village, eventually becoming a street meeting the A35.

2. Walking a short distance to the right will achieve a better sight line to cross the busy road. Go back left past Artwave West Gallery before branching off

121

right towards Whitchurch Canonicorum. Take the first right and then bear left up Pitman's Lane, continuing around the hill as Taylor's Lane later joins from the left.

3. At the high point of the lane, fork off to Ryall along the second of two adjacent paths leaving on the right. After swinging round to the right, watch for a crossing path that climbs very steeply to meet a crossing track. Go right to a junction by a National Trust sign and turn left onto the top of Hardown Hill.

4. Keep ahead with the main track past a radio mast and over the heathy summit. Beyond a bench, the way begins to fall, opening a grand view to Golden Cap and the coast. The track curves down past old chert workings, shortly descending more steeply to a junction. Take the lane on the left, which leads down to the main road.

5. Turn left, crossing to leave after the post office down Shedbush Lane. Through a gate at the bottom, continue beside the right-hand hedge down the edge of a field, dropping out at the bottom by Shedbush Farm via the left-hand of the two field gates. Follow the ongoing track to a junction with Muddyford Lane. Turning right, walk to another junction at its end, known locally as Pickaxe Cross.

6. Following signs to Stonebarrow and Charmouth, take the track ahead, which leads to a farm at Upcot. In the yard, go right, climbing to a junction at the crest of the hill. Keep ahead, shortly passing through a gate to a fork. Bear right with the higher path, which rises around the steep flank of Chardown Hill. Eventually after 0.25 miles (400m), the path passes through a gateway and curves right up to a final gate, exiting onto the top end of the Stonebarrow Hill car park.

Where to eat and drink

Down at Charmouth, at opposite ends of the main street, there's The Royal Oak Inn and The George. Both are open every day and have a good reputation for their food. If you're looking for a café, try the seafront, where you'll find the Charmouth Beach Café, open all day from March to October.

What to see

The attractive thatched buildings of Shedbush Farm were built of local brick and chert cobbles in the 17th century, and include a cider house that brewed apples from the neighbouring orchards. It is now let by the National Trust as a holiday cottage.

While you're there

The seafront around the Cobb at Lyme Regis is one of the most attractive harbour areas along the coast. A medieval port, it became a popular resort during the 18th century, attracting artists and writers, including Turner, Fielding and, of course, Jane Austen, who wrote her novel *Persuasion* while staying there. The beach is also a good place to look for fossils; 12 year-old Mary Anning made history in 1811, when she discovered the fossil of an ichthyosaur in the cliffs.

THE HISTORIC PORT OF LYME REGIS

DISTANCE/TIME	4 miles (6.4km) / 2hrs
ASCENT/GRADIENT	427ft (130m) / ▲ ▲
PATHS	Town centre, promenade, woodland steps, paths
LANDSCAPE	Town, cliffs and hinterland of steep valley
SUGGESTED MAP	AA Walker's Map 11 Lyme Bay
START/FINISH	Grid reference: SY337916
DOG FRIENDLINESS	Very busy in summer, dogs banned from Town Beach March to October; other times on leads
PARKING	Monmouth Beach pay-and-display near harbour (others on route)
PUBLIC TOILETS	Signposted at several car parks and seafront

The Cobb breakwater was first constructed in the 13th century. This sheltered harbour made Lyme Regis Dorset's second largest port. The Cobb was then rebuilt in Portland stone in the early 19th century, with a walkway incorporated on the sheltered side. While the shipping trade had waned by that time, cargoes were still unloaded here into the 20th century. Jane Austen visited Lyme Regis in 1804, and set a pivotal scene of her novel *Persuasion* (1818) on the Cobb – the impetuous Louisa Musgrove mistimed her jump from the steps.

Lyme's main claim to fame is its fossils. The cliffs around the town are rich in Jurassic era sea shells, and important also for discoveries of fossilised fish. Here, in 1811, fisherman's daughter Mary Anning discovered the first complete ichthyosaur – a marine reptile a bit like a dolphin, which could grow up to 33ft (10m) long. This specimen is now the pride of London's Natural History Museum. Few casual amateurs are going to have the pleasure of finding a plesiosaur (also first found here by Mary Anning). The easiest and safest fossils to spot are shells and the Portland Screw (a long, curly gastropod) in the stone flagstones of the Cobb itself. Fragments of ammonites, some as big as dinner plates, can also be spotted in seawashed boulders along Devonshire Beach to west of the Cobb. Both ammonites and the pointed, bullet-like belemnites can be found in the crumbly black rocks of Black Venn, between Lyme and Charmouth. Note that both these beaches are covered at high tide, and the cliffs above are subject to sudden landslips.

Local philanthropist Thomas Hollis created the seafront walkway in 1771 as an alternative to the lower cart road. As you walk along, note the ammonite lamp standards. At the eastern end, the fortifications, Guncliffe Walk, are really a disguise for a modern sewage scheme. Along the seafront, shingle on your left gives way to sand near the amusement arcades. Don't search this beach for fossils: both shingle and sand have been imported, to give the town a beach that's still there even at high tide.

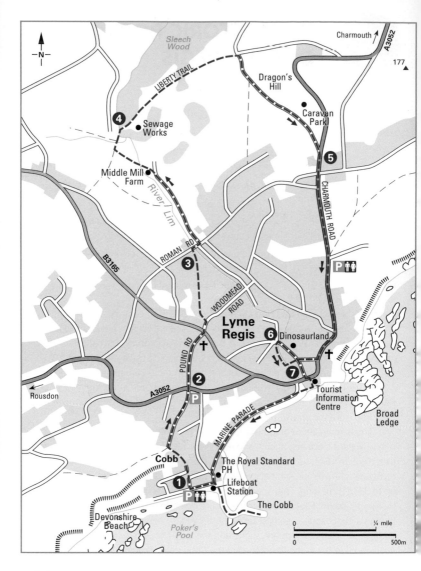

1. From the harbour car park, face inland and take the path that runs to the left of the bowling green, up steps between wooden chalets. Cross a road and continue via more steps up through steep woodland beside a stream. Fork at a kissing gate at the top, then turn right through another kissing gate. Follow first a path and then a road between villas, to lead you across a car park.

2. Cross the road ahead of you and then, with Coram Tower on your left-hand side, continue straight on along Pound Road. Pass the thatched Kersbrook Hotel, then cross the B3165 at Mariners Hotel, to go down Woodmead Road. Immediately turn left through a gate, along the path that carries on down through Slopes Farm woodland. A gate leads out onto Roman Road.

3. Turn right across the River Lim, and turn left up a lane signed 'Wessex Ridgeway'. At a fork, keep ahead on a path to the right of the stream, which it crosses on a footbridge after 220yds (200m). Go through a gate and cross the field ahead. At the corner bear right through a gate, cross a footbridge and bear right over a second one.

4. Near a thatched cottage on the left turn right, signed 'Dragon's Hill', and follow the track up through woods to a gate. Continue past sewage works and through another gate into a field. Go straight on up the hill, with Sleech Wood to your left, into a second field. Near its top, just below Dragon's Hill, go through a gate to a lane corner and turn right, along a hedged track (signposted 'A3052'). It passes along the foot of a caravan park to emerge on the A3052 (Charmouth Road).

5. Turn right and follow this for 0.5 miles (800m), down into the town. Pass the former London pub (now a B&B) and enter the old town. Turn right into Monmouth Street, bearing right through George's Square with its gardens. Keep right, up the hill to the bridge.

6. Take the riverside path down left, signposted 'Town Mill', between mill stream and river. With your back to the Town Mill, go ahead up Mill Lane to Coombe Street – you've visited this corner before! This time turn right down Coombe Street, towards the harbour. At the end turn left on Bridge Street, past the Lyme Fossil Shop and towards the tourist information centre. Turn immediately right between the Guildhall and town museum and descend a flight of stone steps to the shore.

7. Turn right past a huge anchor and continue past an ornate town clock on a small tower to Marine Parade. Continue along the front, eventually passing the Royal Standard pub on your left. Bear left by the Cobb Arms and walk down to the end of the Cobb. Returning, turn left by the Lifeboat Station into the car park.

Where to eat and drink
Lyme's many pubs and cafés are concentrated around Broad Street, the seafront and the harbour area. The traditional Royal Standard pub near the Cobb offers local fish dishes, vegetarian specials and a children's menu with locally sourced ingredients and Palmer's ales from Bridport. There's a sun terrace on the seaward side. Dogs are welcome on a lead.

What to see
Dinosaurland, on Coombe Street in Lyme Regis, is a fascinating fossil museum, with ichthyosaurs, plesiosaurs and other Jurassic delights. Take your own finds to its fossil clinic or go with an expert guide on a fossil walk.

While you're there
For something different, go to sea. Deep-sea fishing trips are offered from Lyme and lots of little boats are available for charter. They advertise a variety of adventures and expeditions on the seafront near the Cobb. There's mackerel fishing in season, too.

BLACK DOWN AND
HARDY MONUMENT

DISTANCE/TIME	7.5 miles (12km) / 3hrs 45min
ASCENT/GRADIENT	820ft (250m) / ▲▲
PATHS	Field tracks, quiet roads, woodland tracks
LANDSCAPE	Rolling hills and escarpments above Abbotsbury
SUGGESTED MAP	AA Walker's Map 5 Weymouth & South Dorset
START/FINISH	Grid reference: SY613876
DOG FRIENDLINESS	Some unfriendly stiles and electric fences
PARKING	By Hardy's Monument, signed off road between Portesham and Winterborne Abbas; also at barrier down east of monument
PUBLIC TOILETS	None on route; nearest toilets are in Back Street, Abbotsbury

Admiral Hardy is remembered today as the friend to whom Lord Nelson addressed his dying words at the Battle of Trafalgar: 'Kiss me, Hardy.' (Or, as perhaps seems more likely, 'Kismet [fate], Hardy.' He was a hero in his own right too, with his features decorating jugs and tankards of the time. Thomas Masterman Hardy was born in 1769 at Kingston Russe, near Long Bredy, and raised at Portesham House in Portesham, under the hill of Black Down. At 15 years of age he slipped secretly aboard a merchantman, where he served before the mast and in the galley before enlisting in the Royal Navy.

Hardy's naval career was illustrious. In 1796, as first lieutenant, he boarded a captured ship when he suddenly saw Nelson's vessel in danger from a Spanish squadron. Hardy hoisted the British flag, drawing the Spanish fire to his own vessel. He was captured, but was later returned in an exchange of prisoners. Some months later a man went overboard from Hardy's ship while he and Nelson were being pursued by a Spanish squadron. Hardy stopped to pick him up, Nelson stopped in support, and their bold action so surprised the Spanish that they broke off their pursuit. Hardy became the captain of Nelson's flagship at many of his most famous battles, including the Nile in 1798. After Nelson's death at Trafalgar, it was Hardy who took command of the fleet. Hardy stayed in the navy for another 30 years. His final service was as Governor of Greenwich Hospital, where he died and was buried in 1839.

Compared to his literary namesake, you'll find few Dorset memorials to this Thomas Hardy, but there is one monument – and it's a big one. Set high on Black Down hill, the Hardy Monument, solid and reliable as Hardy himself, looks like a Victorian chimney. You can climb up inside on summer weekends. Even if it is closed, the views over a sea of green fields and down to Portland are superb.

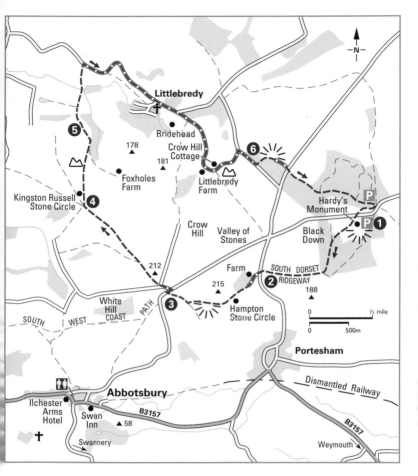

1. From the monument, head to the car park exit but, just before the barrier, turn down left (southwest) opposite a waymark post signed 'Inland Route'. The path crosses a track, and runs down into woods and through a gate. Turn left here along a path to exit between two wooden posts. Turn right along a track, and at once bear left, to cross a stone stile. Cross a wooden stile to walk up the left edges of two fields along an enclosed path that harbours three more stiles. Go over a stone stile and immediately a wooden stile. Bear half left, aiming to the left end of a barn, and leave the field via a gate to a road.

2. Go straight over towards a farm along a track signed 'Abbotsbury Hill Fort'. Go through a gate then another gate to the left of some barns. In 140yds (130m) bear right. Pass Hampton Stone Circle and keep straight on. Go through a field gate and follow the field fence. Go through a galvanised gate beside a field gate (signed 'South Dorset Ridgeway') and continue to the right of a fence, turning right at a gate and stone marker signed 'West Bexington', and turn right up through a gate to a road.

3. Turn right and take the first road left. Soon, at a cattle grid, bear right along a track. In 33yds (30m) keep ahead through a gate (English Heritage marker)

on a grass track to the right of a hedge, fenced off from fields on the right. Follow this through three fields to a track junction.

4. Go ahead through a field gate signed to Kingston Russell Stone Circle, to the stone circle in the field beyond. Pass to the right of it (north) to a small gate in the far fence. Slant steeply downhill (still north), passing right of some grassy earthworks (the remains of prehistoric round huts). At the slope foot follow a fence down to the right, to a gate in an electric fence. Through this, bear left along a track, with the fence to your left, for 200yds (180m) to a gate.

5. Down through this gate keep ahead to a hedge, and turn right alongside it. Halfway down the field, turn right and cut across it, to a small gate in the opposite hedge. Cross a ditch and stream, and keep ahead to join the hedge along the field top. At this field's end, cross a double stile, and contour forward (east), then drop gently to cross a footbridge. Head up through the streamside trees, then slant up to the right to a stile. Head uphill, parallel with the road that's at the field top, soon seeing Littlebredy Church ahead. Cross the final field, then take a path passing to the right of the church. Go left through a gate and turn right onto the road. In 110yds (100m) bear right at a cycle route sign. Continue past Crow Hill Cottage and up a long hill to a road junction.

6. Turn right for 300yds (275m). Just after a bridleway signpost, turn sharp left onto a green track. This bends right to become a mud path beside some woods and past a barn. Cross the road and go straight ahead, to the left of the woods. The wide path descends into the woods and divides: here turn up to the right. The path runs above the top edge of the woods, joining a track to reach the roadside below the Hardy Monument. Turn right, and take a rising path to the right of the road to reach the monument.

Where to eat and drink

Abbotsbury is well supplied with tea rooms. On Market Street, The Old Schoolhouse offers home-made cakes. The Abbotsbury Tea Rooms has a garden and welcomes dogs, while Abbey House near the church also has a tea room and garden. If you want something stronger, the Ilchester Arms and the Swan Inn both have beer gardens.

What to see

There are two prehistoric stone circles on this walk. The first is Hampton Stone Circle, where the nine stone lumps are used by cattle as scratching posts. The stone of the circle is a natural phenomenon, with flint gravel cemented by silica, laid down over 40 million years ago. The numerous lumps of the Kingston Russell Stone Circle are mottled with lichen.

While you're there

Abbotsbury Swannery is a unique sanctuary. Mute swans have lived on the Fleet for 600 years, since they were introduced as a food source for the abbey, and their nest site is now protected. Come in April to see them nesting and from mid-May to see cygnets. The tithe barn nearby houses the Abbotsbury Children's Farm. Just outside the village are the Subtropical Gardens.

LAWRENCE OF ARABIA'S RETREAT AT CLOUDS HILL

DISTANCE/TIME	6 miles (9.7km) / 2hrs 30min
ASCENT/GRADIENT	279ft (85m) / ▲
PATHS	Heathland tracks, forest, field and woodland paths
LANDSCAPE	Open heath, woodland beside army training area, village
SUGGESTED MAP	AA Walker's Map 5 Weymouth & South Dorset
START/FINISH	Grid reference: SY826904
DOG FRIENDLINESS	May need lifting over some stiles due to rabbit fencing
PARKING	Car park on road between Bovington Camp and Clouds Hill
PUBLIC TOILETS	No public toilets but some at Walled Garden, Moreton (donation welcome)

Captain T E Lawrence continues to fascinate, thanks in part to David Lean's iconic 1962 film, *Lawrence of Arabia*. Thomas Edward Lawrence was born in 1888 in North Wales. As an Oxford undergraduate he undertook a 1,100-mile (1,769km) walking tour of Palestine and Syria, collecting material for a thesis on Crusader castles. He went on to work as an archaeologist in Syria, and took odd jobs on wanderings throughout the Middle East and Greece. He gained a knowledge of Arab life that was invaluable during World War I, when he was posted to military intelligence in Cairo. Lawrence was a leader with a driving personality and deep knowledge of strategic warfare. His courage and adoption of Arabic dress made him a heroic figure, seized on by the press of the day as Aqaba, in Jordan, was captured in 1917, and Damascus the following year.

Lawrence remained involved in Arab affairs after the war, lobbying unsuccessfully for Arab independence. Finding fame a millstone and dissatisfied with what he described as 'the shallow grave of public duty', he joined the RAF in 1922, seeking a regular life as Aircraftsman Ross. But he was discovered, so he joined the Tank Corps at Bovington in 1923 as Private T E Shaw, and moved to Dorset, where he bought the house at Clouds Hill as a retreat. It is a bachelor house, surrounded by rhododendrons, with well-stocked book shelves, a gramophone, comfortable firesides and few frills. It became his 'earthly paradise'. He finished writing his account of the Arab Revolt, *The Seven Pillars of Wisdom* (1926), here, and made friends with Thomas Hardy, then living in Dorchester. In 1925 Lawrence rejoined the RAF, helping to develop and test the speedboats of the fledgling air-sea rescue service. In 1935 he retired to Clouds Hill. However, on 13 May that year he went out to send a telegram. Returning on his Brough Superior SS-100, he swerved to avoid cyclists and was thrown from the motorbike. He died five days later at the age of 46 and was buried in Moreton churchyard.

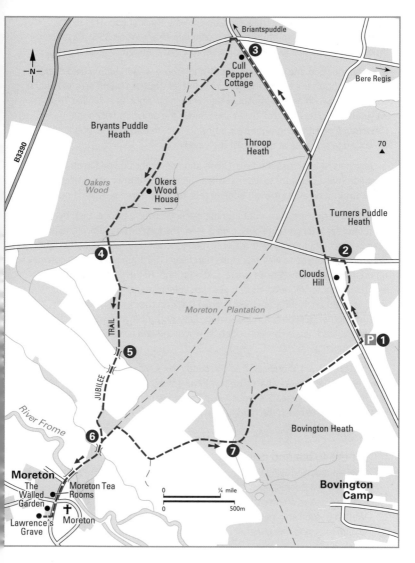

1. At the corner of the car park, a memorial stone marks where Lawrence was fatally injured. Behind it, take a path signed for Clouds Hill, running to the right of the road. Soon you pass a second, older memorial stone. The path becomes sandy and heads uphill by the fence. Bushes screen Clouds Hill, to the left. Keep right, round the fence, and bear left to the road.

2. Turn sharp left along the verge, then at the junction cross the road on your right, to a waymarked path across Turners Puddle Heath Nature Reserve, a Site of Special Scientific Interest (SSSI). Go through a gate at the other side and walk up the road opposite, to pass Cull Pepper Cottage to a junction.

3. Turn left ('Affpuddle') for 50yds (45m). Opposite a second branch of the road from the north, turn left again on a firm path across Bryants Puddle Heath.

Keep straight on where a track crosses onto the track ahead. This leads (southwest, bending south) through a gate into Okers Wood SSSI. Pass Okers Wood House and join its drive, which bends right then left to meet a road.

4. Cross the road and go straight on through more woods, with a field opening on your right. At the end of the field bear left for 150yds (140m) on a woodland path. As the woodland opens out to tall pines, bear right, at a Jubilee Trail waymarker. Follow the trail as it winds under the pines then through rhododendrons, bearing right over a tiny stream, to duckboards and finally a footbridge and stile at the end of the woods.

5. Bear half right across the field. Cross another footbridge and keep the same direction (west of south) to a Jubilee Trail sign at the corner of a fenced copse. Head straight on along the left edge of this large field to a stile and fingerpost.

6. Cross the stile and turn right into the track. Go over a bridge, then bear right to cross a long bridge over a ford. Pass the former post office and a side road on the right to reach a three-way road junction (tea rooms on the right). Walk straight ahead to visit Moreton churchyard (through a porticoed gateway on the right) with Lawrence's grave at the far end. Return past the junction and turn right for Moreton church. Retrace your route to waypoint 6 and keep straight on. In 150yds (140m) take a track on the right ('Bovington') and, in another 300yds (275m), bear left (Lawrence of Arabia waymark). The broad track leads through a gate in woodland and across the heath to another junction.

7. Turn left, signed 'Clouds Hill' up the sandy track. Where it divides turn right (Lawrence of Arabia waymark), up hill. Where the track ends at the top of the hill, the range path ahead is fenced in, with yellow markers. It runs to the left of a tank track, to reach the road just left of the car park.

Where to eat and drink

The old diamond-windowed schoolhouse in Moreton now houses the Moreton Tea Rooms, open from 10am to 5pm for home-made daily specials, cakes, fresh sandwiches, ice creams and cold drinks. The Walled Garden also has a very fine café, serving brunch, lunch and cream teas, and has gluten-free, vegetarian and vegan options.

What to see

Don't miss the breathtaking windows in Moreton church. The church itself was rebuilt after severe bomb damage in 1940. What looks like plain glass from the outside, from the inside is revealed to be engraved with a vivid flow of delicate pictorial designs.

While you're there

The Walled Garden at Moreton (donation welcome) contains all manner of different gardens within it, as well as a garden shop, vineyard, nursery and café. It is maintained by horticulture students working with Employ My Ability, which specialises in training people with special needs.

WAREHAM FOREST

DISTANCE/TIME	6 miles (9.6km) / 2hrs 15min
ASCENT/GRADIENT	250ft (78m) / ▲
PATHS	Clear woodland tracks and paths
LANDSCAPE	Pine forest and wetland heath
SUGGESTED MAP	AA Walker's Map 5 Weymouth & South Dorset
START/FINISH	Grid reference: SY906893
DOG FRIENDLINESS	Under close control because of deer and nesting birds
PARKING	Sika Trail car park (free), beside minor road 1 mile (1.6km) northwest of Wareham
PUBLIC TOILETS	None on route

Extending over 14 square miles (36km²), Wareham forest encompasses both wood and lowland heath. It was one of many forests planted by the newly formed Forestry Commission after World War I, which had exposed the country's strategic lack of timber; vast quantities had been used in shoring trenches and as pit props in the coal mines.

Early planting relied on fast-cropping species and resulted in conifer blankets that were visually unappealing and provided almost no wildlife habitat. But after war again depleted the country's timber reserve, the strategy began to change, introducing a variety of species, including broad-leaved trees, and developing an increasing awareness of environmental issues and the importance of habitat variety.

Wareham Forest today is both productive and sustains a huge diversity of wildlife. Among the tree species are several varieties of pine as well as larch and oak, with birch, hazel, holly and other trees established around the plantation fringes. The ongoing cycle of planting, thinning and felling creates a rotating pattern of open space that allows wildflowers and heath plants to develop, while the lowland mire at its heart is one of the largest such areas in Britain.

The largest animals roaming the forest are deer, of which there are three species: sika, roe and fallow. Roe deer are native, while fallow deer were re-introduced by both the Romans and the Normans. Sika arrived from the Far East during the late 19th century, escapees from private parks and now so successful that numbers have to be controlled. There are plenty of foxes and badgers and occasional sightings of otter, but less obvious are dormice, which were originally thought to live only in ancient woodland.

The area is particularly important for reptiles and is one of the few places where you might see all six of Britain's native reptiles: adder, grass snake, smooth snake, sand lizard, common lizard and slow worm. The smooth snake is secretive and although sometimes superficially resembling an adder, is not venomous, subduing its prey by constriction. Sand lizards are much larger than the common lizard and, like them, might be seen basking in the sun. The male is readily identifiable by having green flanks, which become prominent during the breeding season.

The woodland is rich in birdlife, including woodpeckers, treecreepers and crossbills as well as birds of prey such as red kites, buzzards and hen harriers. The heath is one of the strongholds of the Dartford warbler and on summer evenings you may hear a nightjar.

Among the plants to look out for around the marsh are bog asphodel, its yellow flowers once collected to make hair dye, and the sundew, a carnivorous plant that traps and absorbs nutrients from insects.

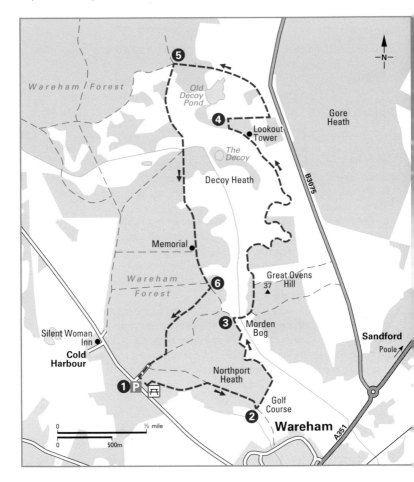

1. Look for a tall Sika 'Red Trail' marker near the far-right corner of the car park by picnic tables. Walk through the trees to a bridle gate and, following red markers, go right on a broad swathe. As it later curves left at the forest edge, ignore a path off right and carry on back into trees to a major crossroads. Go right and carry on to a junction in front of a boundary gate.

2. Swinging left, head down beside the boundary. At the bottom of the hill, the trail curves left at the edge of Morden Bog.

3. Reaching a junction of tracks by a dark pool, abandon the red markers and turn right. Entering the National Nature Reserve, cross a stream. As the trail curves left, ignore a track right. The way gently rises across Great Ovens Hill, from where there is an extensive view across the marsh and surrounding forest. Rounding a bend, watch for a track forking down left by a bench to continue around the convoluted perimeter of the bog. Carry on for 1.5 miles (2.4km), eventually passing a lookout tower perched at the edge of the forest plantation. Just beyond, the track turns in along a break between the trees to meet a crossing track, a short distance south of the Old Decoy Pond.

4. Turn right. Approaching a gate at the eastern edge of the plantation, swing left beside a wire fence. After 200yds (183m), the path curves gently left. Keep left at a fork and carry on above the northern edge of the Old Decoy Pond. Ignore a couple of tracks leaving on the right towards the higher ground, soon arriving at a crossing path at the edge of trees.

5. Go left and keep straight on at the next junction, later crossing a bridge and reaching a fork. Stick with the branch ahead and carry on for another half-mile (800m) to a junction beside a memorial stone at Parson's Pleasure. Continue forward, shortly passing another junction to reach a red-topped waypost, 100yds (91m) further on, marking a narrow path off to the right.

6. Rising from the bog, the path undulates into the forest. Later reaching a fork, take the left branch and climb to a broad trail. Still following red-topped wayposts, go right and then immediately left, rising to a second trail. Follow that right, shortly arriving at a junction in front of a couple of gates. Pass through the smaller bridle gate on the left, from which a path winds through the trees back to the car park.

Where to eat and drink

The nearby Silent Woman Inn was reputedly a haunt for smugglers, who cut out the landlady's tongue so that she couldn't betray them. Today, apart from Mondays when it is closed, there's plenty of lively chat and you can get anything from a light bite to a three-course meal.

What to see

Look out for bat nesting boxes. The forest supports eight species of bat, including the pipistrelle, Britain's smallest bat, which can consume 3,000 insects in a single night. The bats are best seen as dusk falls.

While you're there

Although born at Tremadog in North Wales, Thomas Edward Lawrence (Lawrence of Arabia) retired to Clouds Hill, just north of Bovington Camp. The house is now cared for by the National Trust and contains many of his possessions. Lawrence died aged only 46 in 1935, from head injuries sustained in a motorcycle accident and is buried in the churchyard at nearby Moreton.

HENGISTBURY HEAD COASTAL LOOP

DISTANCE/TIME	3.25 miles (5.3km) / 1hr 30min
ASCENT/GRADIENT	109ft (33m) / ▲▲
PATHS	Grass, tarmac road, soft sand, woodland track, some steps
LANDSCAPE	Heathland, sand cliffs, sand spit, mixed woodland
SUGGESTED MAP	AA Walker's Map 6 Poole, Bournemouth & Purbeck
START/FINISH	Grid reference: SZ163912
DOG FRIENDLINESS	Keep to paths to avoid destroying habitat and disturbing ground-nesting birds
PARKING	Car park (fee) at end of road, signed 'Hengistbury Head' from B3059; parking is also permitted on the approach road to the car park, but both road and car park are gated and locked daily at 10pm
PUBLIC TOILETS	Beside car park; also amid beach huts

The multi-coloured beach huts of Mudeford's sandy peninsula are a throwback to bucket-and-spade holidays of the early 20th century. In fact, they hark back to the last days of the century before that, when bathers would undress in modest little huts on wheels, which could be horse-hauled down into the shallows in order to minimise any embarrassing exposure to public view.

Those days are long gone, but the carriages' successors, the huts, are still there, and the desire for one's own bit of space right on the beach remains undiminished. Candy-striped paintwork has given way to soft, colour-washed hues, but the urge to individualise remains strong, with decks, weathervanes and windmilling, semaphoring sailors. While the huts' outer form remains much the same – central door, symmetrical windows, shallow, peaked roof – the insides vary wildly. Some make the most of one light, airy space reflecting sparkling sea and sky; others may be divided into rooms, with perhaps a sleeping platform squeezed up under the roof. Each is customised with its owner's particular beach 'necessities' – minimalist fridge and drinks cabinet in one, kitchen sink and home comforts in another. Names may reflect the owners' identities but all express an air of relaxation and fun: for example whimsical Jangles next to Hideaway, and Ar Lan Y Mor, from a Welsh folk song that speaks of love beside the sea.

The windswept peninsula of Hengistbury Head has an archaeological record dating back 12,500 years, when Stone Age hunter-gatherers left the remains of a camp site on its outer, seaward edge. Some 10,500 years later Iron Age folk settled here and built up a trading port on the more sheltered inner shore, where Barn Field stands today. The great Double Dikes date from this later period, built to shelter timber-framed dwellings. Barn Field itself has remained untouched by farming improvements since the Romans left around AD 410 – a rare status protected by conservationists, especially on this crowded south coast. Its vegetation is low, acidic grassland that grips onto thin soil over gravel and sand, maintained down the centuries by salt-laden winds and the sharp teeth of the rabbit population. Decimation of the rabbits in the 1950s by myxomatosis allowed gorse and bramble to gain a hold, but scrub clearance and controlled grazing by cattle have done much to restore the original balance. Today it is an important site for ground-nesting birds, adorned with the flowers of heath bedstraw, autumn hawkbit and heath speedwell.

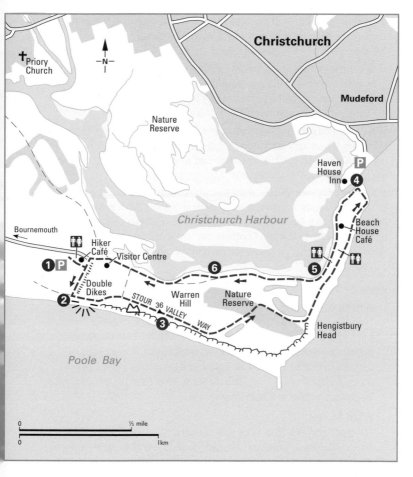

1. From the corner of the car park take the gravel path towards the sea, with the fenced-off lines of the Double Dikes to your left. At the sea-edge you can see for miles each way: to the towers of Bournemouth, the chalky Foreland and Durlston Head to the west, Christchurch Bay and the Isle of Wight to the east.

2. Turn left and follow the road along the cliffs. The Priory Church in Christchurch dominates the view inland across the harbour, with St Catherine's Hill behind. Follow the road up the hill. Pause to inspect the boggy pond on your right, home to the rare natterjack toad. The road narrows; climb up some steps, passing a numbered post ('33') marking the Stour Valley

Way. As you climb the steep path, the views back along the coast are fabulous, and there are views across the shallows of Christchurch Harbour, usually buzzing with windsurfers and sailing dinghies.

3. On the heathy top of Warren Hill a viewing platform tells you that you're 75 miles (120km) from Cherbourg and 105 miles (168km) from Jersey. Keep right along the path, passing a deserted coastguard station and following the top of the cliffs. Descend (forking right) into a deep hollow, where the sea appears to be breaking through; this pool is called Quarry Pond. Keep straight on, following the curve of the head. At the end the path turns down through some trees; descend the steps. Walk along the sparkling, white sand on the sea side of the beach huts to the point. Stone groynes form little bays.

4. At the end of the spit you're only a stone's throw from the opposite shore (a ferry runs across to the pub from the end of a pier, passed further on). Turn round the end of the point, passing the old Black House, and walk up the inner side of the spit, overlooking the harbour.

5. If you've had enough beach, you can catch the land train back to the car park from here (times vary seasonally – call the Hiker Café on 01202 428552 for details). Otherwise, join the metalled road which curves round to the right past the freshwater marsh and lagoon.

6. At a post marked '19' turn right onto the dirt path and follow it briefly through the woods, crossing a small ditch on a short plank bridge, to emerge back on the road. Turn right, passing extensive reedbeds on the right and a bird sanctuary on the left. Continue past the thatched Hengistbury Head Visitor Centre and follow the road to the café, ranger station building and car park.

Where to eat and drink

The Hiker Café beside the car park serves hot meals, soup and sandwiches. There's also the pleasant Beach House Café on the spit, overlooking Christchurch Harbour (no dogs inside). It has a bar and specialises in pizzas and exotic panini. The Hengistbury Head Visitor Centre (open summer from 10am to 5pm), 200m from the car park, sells ice creams and hot and cold drinks.

What to see

The rare natterjack toad, once widespread on the heaths and coastal dunes of England, has been squeezed down to just 50 breeding sites, one of which is the little boggy pond on Hengistbury Head.

While you're there

Christchurch's Priory Church dominates the view inland and is well worth exploring. Nearby Place Mill, mentioned in the Domesday Book, was used for fulling (cleaning and thickening cloth) and corn grinding until 1808. Don't miss Christchurch's ducking stool, reached via a flagged alleyway beside Ye Olde George Inn. It's a wooden stool on the end of a pole which can be dipped into the millstream.

STUDLAND BEACH AND HEATH

DISTANCE/TIME	7 miles (11.3km) / 3hrs 30min
ASCENT/GRADIENT	132ft (40m) / Negligible
PATHS	Sandy beach, muddy heathland tracks, verges
LANDSCAPE	Sandy Studland Bay, heath and views over Poole Harbour
SUGGESTED MAP	AA Walker's Map 5 Weymouth & South Dorset
START/FINISH	Grid reference: SZ033835
DOG FRIENDLINESS	Dogs on leads are allowed on the beach from May to September
PARKING	Knoll Beach car park (fee), by visitor centre just off B3351
PUBLIC TOILETS	By visitor centre and near ferry toll station

The glorious sands in Studland Bay are justly famous, attracting over one million visitors a year, so you'll need to get up early to have the beach to yourself. You're unlikely to be alone for long, and local horse-riders are often the first to arrive. As you progress up the beach, getting warmer, you can shed your clothes with impunity, for the upper stretch is the less familiar form of nature reserve, opening its arms to naturists. Even on a winter's morning you'll spot brave souls sunbathing naked in the shelter of the marram-covered dunes. Offshore you'll see big, sleek motor boats – of the 'gin palace' variety – letting rip as they emerge from the constraints of Poole Harbour. Watch out, too, for the orange and blue of the Poole lifeboat on manoeuvres, and the yellow and black pilot boat nipping out to lead in the tankers. Jet-skiers zip around the more sedate sailing yachts, all dodging the small fishing boats. It's a perfect seaside harmony, complete with wheeling gulls.

Studland's sand is pale gold and fine-ground, trodden by thousands of feet, piled into hundreds of satisfying sandcastles and smoothed daily by the sea. The shells underfoot become more numerous as you approach the tip of the sand bar. It's a wonderful opportunity for some shell-spotting. Behind the beach lies the rugged heath, part of the same nature reserve, which is in the care of the National Trust. The Trust is reclaiming heath that had become farmland, clearing scrub and maintaining controlled grazing to prevent it all reverting to woodland. Some of the heath is still recovering after a disastrous fire in 2009. You might spot a rare Dartford warbler here – with its pinky-brown colouring and long tail, it's a distinctive little bird. All six of Britain's reptiles – common lizard, sand lizard, smooth snake, adder, grass snake and slow worm – live on the heath. Be patient and you might see one soaking up the sunshine in a quiet corner. Trapped between the dunes and the heath is a freshwater lake known as the Little Sea. Hides allow you to watch the dizzying variety of coastal and freshwater birds which congregate here.

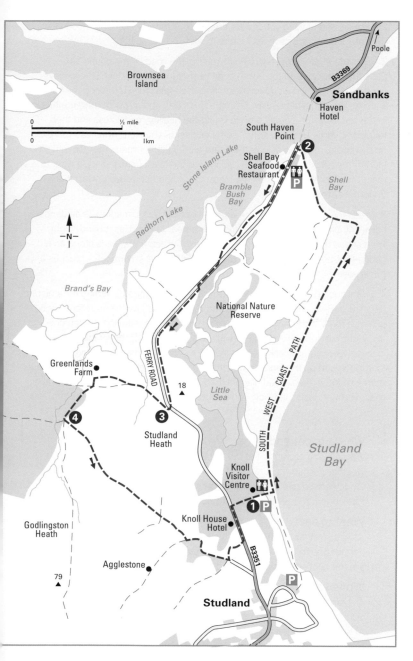

1. From the car park go past the visitor centre to the sea. Turn left and walk up the beach for about 2 miles (3.2km). Marram-covered dunes hide the heath on your left, but you have views to the Isle of Wight, and the golden cliffs of Bournemouth curve away ahead. Continue round the tip of the sand bar into Shell Bay. Poole opens out ahead – more precisely, the spit of Sandbanks, with

the Haven Hotel facing you across the harbour mouth. There are good views of the nature reserve Brownsea Island.

2. Turn inland at South Haven Point, joining the road by the phone box. Pass the boatyard and toll booth, then bear right at a barrier ('Emergency Exit') on a track leading down to some houseboats. Turn left along the inner shore of Poole Harbour. After Bramble Bush Bay and a row of concrete blocks in the sea, bear left on any path to rejoin the nearby road. Cross and then follow the verge until the end of some woods on your left, when you can pick up the broad, muddy track on the heath alongside the road. After 0.5 miles (800m) the track and road bend left. Where the track bends sharply right to meet the road, stay ahead on the footpath for another 100yds (90m) to a fingerpost at the roadside.

3. Cross the road into the right-hand one of two tracks, marked 'Greenlands Farm'. At a junction near Greenlands Farm bear left and, as it bends right, keep ahead through a gate on to the heath. A green track leads along an old hedge-line, past a large shed on the left, and 175yds (160m) later reaches a fingerpost.

4. Go through the gate ahead and turn half left (southeast), aiming for a distant fingerpost. Bear slightly left, as indicated ('Studland') by the fingerpost, soon joining a flinty track. It crosses the moorland rise, passing the Agglestone away to your right. Blue bridleway arrows mark the way down into some woods. Keep left at a fork just before the woods, then bear right over a footbridge and up through a gate into a lane. Pass a house, then turn left (blue markers) into a field. Head diagonally right into a green lane leading to the road. Turn left past the Knoll House Hotel, then right to return to the car park.

Where to eat and drink

The café and restaurant at the Knoll Visitor Centre is open year-round, weather permitting. A range of home-made food is on offer, from all-day breakfasts to soup and light lunches. The Shell Bay Seafood Restaurant at South Haven Point has great views from its terrace.

What to see

As you stroll along the beach, look back to the chalky cliffs of the Foreland, with the white arches and stacks of Old Harry Rocks. They are the opposite end of the Needles (at the tip of the Isle of Wight).

While you're there

A chain ferry crosses every few minutes between Sandbanks and South Haven Point, disgorging its 'townies' on to the beach and its cars to hurry off into Portland. From Sandbanks you can catch a ferry from mid-March to late October to Brownsea Island. Red squirrels are the best-known inhabitants of this 500-acre (200ha) nature reserve, but the lagoon supports an important ternery, and avocets, ruff and other unusual waders are visitors. There are many other rare creatures, including 17 species of dragonfly and an endangered species of ant.

THE BLUE POOL

DISTANCE/TIME	3.5 miles (5.7km) / 1hr 45min
ASCENT/GRADIENT	165ft (50m) / ▲
PATHS	Country lanes, heath and woodland tracks (may be boggy)
LANDSCAPE	Heath, woodland, rolling country
SUGGESTED MAP	AA Walker's Map 5 Weymouth & South Dorset
START/FINISH	Grid reference: SY931837
DOG FRIENDLINESS	Some road walking; on lead in the Blue Pool reserve and on heath to east of Cotness Farm where deer abound
PARKING	At roadside just south of phone box in Furzebrook
PUBLIC TOILETS	None on route, unless visiting the Blue Pool

Until quite recently, Furzebrook's roads were stained white by lorries from the clay pits: the village was once the centre for the Dorset extraction of ball clay. This is a clay formed of particularly fine, uniform particles, useful for many sorts of pottery, from fine white teapots to toilet bowls and basins. Dorset and Devon have some of the world's most important deposits.

Furzebrook is an unremarkable estate village of Victorian houses, while Furzebrook House is once more a private home. Commandeered during World War II, it was in such poor shape by the end of it that the owners, the Barnards, refused to take it back. It became, instead, a government research establishment, which it remained for years. The Blue Pool is a beauty spot on the Furzebrook Estate. It was first opened to the public by T T Barnard in 1935, and is owned by his daughter today. Gloriously set amid trees, the pool itself is an old clay pit filled with rainwater, and it is the minute ball-clay particles suspended in the water that refract the sunlight and give the pool its deep turquoise colour. The body of water is at its most vivid on a cold, grey day. At other times it appears emerald green.

There are lots of woodland paths to explore, as well as an adventure playground for children and a museum of the clay industry. You can enjoy the beautiful setting on this walk, whether or not the pool itself is open. The heathland, woodland and open water, all undisturbed for more than 50 years, were in 1985 designated a Site of Special Scientific Interest (SSSI). There are areas of ancient oakwood, with lush secondary growth on the abandoned clay workings. Deer (including the tiny Sika), badgers, grey squirrels and dragonflies are common here, as are bears – the Wareham miniature teddy bears in their own 15-room house. Luckier sightings could include the green-coloured sand lizard and smooth snake, plus birds such as the Dartford warbler. Rare in the UK as a whole, marsh gentians are fairly common here. Look out for them between July and October.

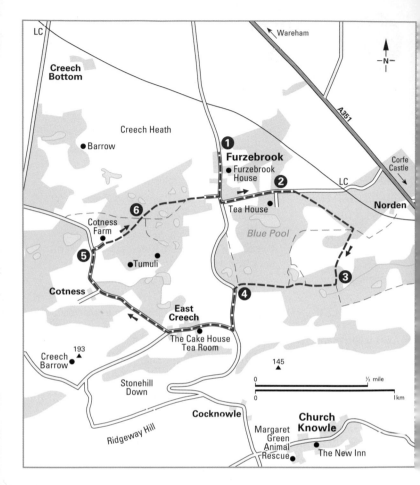

1. Walk south on the main road through the village, passing the drive to Furzebrook House on your left. At the end of the park wall turn left down a drive, signed to the Blue Pool. After a parking area (for paying visitors), pass the entrance to the Blue Pool on your right.

2. Continue ahead (signed 'Purbeck Way') into the woods. Stay on the main track (marked 'Purbeck Way and Corfe Castle'; ignore a path to the left), to go through a kissing gate onto the heath. In 30yds (27m), at a marker stone ('Purbeck Way'), bear right off the track onto a peaty path through gorse and heather (southeast). At the heath edge go through another kissing gate. At a marker stone signed 'F.P. to Corfe', turn right over the duckboard walkway. The wet path leads you (southwest) through pretty woodland dripping with moss and lichen. Cross a sleeper bridge over an orange-stained marsh. After a pool on your left, continue along the boundary fence and further duckboards.

3. At a junction of paths (with bridges to your left) go straight on, following the blue marker, signposted 'East Creech'. Pass a reedy pool on your left on the broad path up through the woods. Ignore any side paths to the right, and keep on the main path (west), marked for East Creech, to a road.

4. Turn left, past the turning for East Creech Farm camp site, to a junction. Turn right here, up the road into East Creech village. At the end, keep right at a left turning. The quiet valley road passes woods and Creech Barrow Hill, both on your left. It rises steadily to pass thatched Cotness Cottages, again on the left. As the road starts to descend there are views over the Isle of Purbeck, with Wareham ahead.

5. Turn right along the driveway of Cotness Farm, and before the farm gate cross a stile to the right. Cross the narrow part of the field ahead and turn left along the foot of the woods, down the field to cross a stile at its corner. Turn half left away from the fence, through laurel and rhododendron, and then on a faint path (northeast) across the heath, through trees and gorse.

6. At a waymarker (yellow arrow), cross over two tracks to join a track, bending to the right (east). After a kissing gate the track runs through birches, with bracken below. Pass between a shed and a garden fence, then pass a house on your right and walk straight ahead to meet the road. Turn left and retrace your steps through Furzebrook to the start.

Where to eat and drink

The Tea House has operated since the Blue Pool first opened. The barn-based Cake House Tea Room in East Creech is a much more recent undertaking and makes an admirable place to stop for light refreshments. For a pub or in winter, try the venerable hostelry The New Inn at nearby Church Knowle. The restaurant specialises in fish and there's a beer garden at the rear. Dogs are not allowed inside, but are welcome in the garden.

What to see

Clay dug here in the 17th century was used in the manufacture of clay pipes and later as a component in the manufacture of china, most notably at Wedgwood in Staffordshire. This story is told in the little museum by the Blue Pool.

While you're there

On the western edge of the village of Church Knowle is a different sort of retirement centre – it's the extensive Margaret Green Animal Rescue, where domestic, farm and wild animals come to retire, or to find a new home. There's even an aviary for lost, injured or oiled birds. Admission is by donation and there's a gift shop to help support the sanctuary's work.

THE WHITE HORSE AT OSMINGTON

DISTANCE/TIME	4 miles (6.4km) / 2hrs
ASCENT/GRADIENT	568ft (173m) / ▲ ▲
PATHS	Farm and village lanes, woodland paths, field paths
LANDSCAPE	Sheltered green valley behind coastline and chalky ridge of White Horse Hill
SUGGESTED MAP	AA Walker's Map 5 Weymouth & South Dorset
START/FINISH	Grid reference: SY724829
DOG FRIENDLINESS	On leads when passing livestock
PARKING	Church Lane in Osmington, just off A353
PUBLIC TOILETS	None on route

The 1994 film *The Madness of King George* did much to remind the world of a monarch whose identity had been obscured by time. In the Dorset town of Weymouth, however, he has never been forgotten. Weymouth is a trading port with a proximity to France that had left it vulnerable to raids. The town found new life in the 18th century as a base for trade with the Americas and the shipping of convicts to Australia. The 1780s saw the emergence of the cult of sea bathing (even seawater drinking), and Weymouth joined in. A royal visit in 1789, however, was to rocket the little town to the top rank of seaside resorts.

Rumours of George III's mental instability were threatening to destabilise the country. Accordingly, it was decided that the King should go on a short and highly visible tour, to enable his subjects to see how much better he was. Weymouth was picked, and a six-day journey commenced for the royal party, which consisted of the King, the Queen and three princesses. It was a great build-up and, by the time they reached Weymouth, the crowds were ecstatic, with bunting, mayoral receptions and gunships firing salutes. The King responded with a short walkabout on his very first evening and the declaration that he 'never saw a sight so pleasing'.

Any hopes that the King might have had of a quiet dip in the sea, however, were dashed a week later by the strength of local enthusiasm for the royal visitor. Even as his royal-crested bathing hut was being wheeled into the sea, a band hidden in a nearby bathing machine were waiting to burst into a loyal song as soon as the regal body hit the water. George III spent ten weeks here on his first visit, enjoying day trips to Lulworth, Milton Abbey and St Aldhelm's Head, and sailing off Portland. The royal family returned two years later for a holiday and then returned every year until 1805. In 1808 John Rainier arranged for a symbol of the town's loyalty and gratitude for the royal attention to be carved into the chalk downs above Osmington. A silhouette of the King on horseback was created, 324ft (99m) high, riding away from the town. Once clearly visible from Weymouth, Portland and ships out at sea, today the chalk figure is weathered and grey, but otherwise in very good condition.

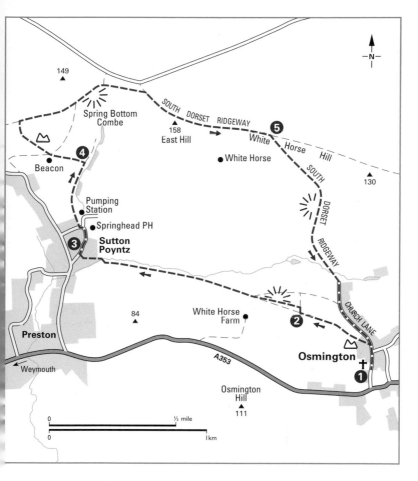

1. From Osmington church walk down the village street of pretty thatched cottages. At the junction keep on down Church Lane. Opposite The Cartshed turn left up a steep flight of steps. The path then bears right and undulates through the trees. Cross a stile and continue straight along the hedge to the end of a field.

2. Cross a stile and turn right down through a hedge gap, and immediately climb a stile on the left. Slant down the field to a stile in the far bottom corner, meanwhile looking to your right to see the White Horse. Turn left, crossing a farm track, and go through a gate by a stile. Cross the next field to its far bottom corner, beside a stream. Cross a stile and an earth ditch (parish boundary). Continue along the bottoms of two fields, next to the largely hidden stream. Cross a track to a gate, and through it follow a track ahead, which bends right to cross the stream. At once go through a small gate on the left. Continue towards Sutton Poyntz, taking a gate and then a path to the village street.

3. Turn right, passing the Mill House and the tall, red-brick mill on your left. Pass the village pond and just after the Springhead pub on the right, turn left

along Mission Hall Lane and then right up a track past Springfield Cottage. Go through a gate with a pumping station on the right, and continue ahead. After the next gate, carry on along the track to just below the entrance to steep Spring Bottom Combe.

4. Cross a stile by a gate and turn left up a raking, grassy track. It passes a beacon erected in 2005 for the bicentenary of the Battle of Trafalgar. At the top of the steep slope, go through a gate and bear right beside a phone wire up to a hedge, and turn right along the scarp top. (From here you'll follow signs 'South Dorsetshire Ridgeway' back to Osmington.) Along the green track you pass numerous tumuli, or prehistoric burial mounds, with great views along the valley and down to Weymouth Bay and Portland. Through a gate at the head of Spring Bottom Combe, keep ahead to pass a tumulus with a dew pond, and take a narrow gate on the left to join a track signposted for Osmington. Soon this passes a trig point. Go through a gate and keep straight on, with a good view to strip lynchets (terraces) on the hillside ahead.

5. After the next gate bear down to the right, signed 'Osmington'. The track leads down the hill, through a gate – look back to see the White Horse again. Follow the lane back up through the village to your car.

Where to eat and drink

The Springhead pub in Sutton Poyntz is beside the village pond and fairly buzzes on summer weekends. There's a beer garden and a children's play area. Dogs are welcome in the bar and at the tables outside the front of the pub. It serves a good range of bar food and has a more substantial restaurant menu.

What to see

As you walk along White Horse Hill there is a clear view of terracing on the grassy slopes of the combe ahead. These are strip lynchets, relics of a farming system introduced in the 12th and 13th centuries in Dorset, to maximise cultivable land.

While you're there

The seaside town of Weymouth has a long beach and an appealing, old seafront promenade, complete with lacy, wrought-iron decoration. Apart from the usual seaside amusements, attractions include historic Nothe Fort, and a fascinating time walk through a Victorian brewery, combined with craft outlets and specialist shopping at Brewer's Quay, on the Old Harbour.

AN ABBOTSBURY LOOP

DISTANCE/TIME	4.5 miles (7.2km) / 2hrs
ASCENT/GRADIENT	800ft (244m) / ▲ ▲
PATHS	Field paths and tracks, a short distance along lanes
LANDSCAPE	Rolling downs
SUGGESTED MAP	AA Walker's Map 5 Weymouth & South Dorset
START/FINISH	Grid reference: SY578852
DOG FRIENDLINESS	Dogs on leads near grazing livestock
PARKING	Pay car park in Abbotsbury
PUBLIC TOILETS	In Abbotsbury village

Abbotsbury overlooks the head of The Fleet, a long, salty lagoon separated from the sea by the high shingle bank backing Chesil Beach. The sheltered lake and surrounding reeds provided ideal nesting, and the monks of the nearby 11th-century Benedictine monastery learned how to manage mute swans and other birds as a source of meat. Today the swannery comprises around 600 birds and is a nature reserve and popular visitor attraction.

Legend has it that a church predating the abbey was founded by Bertulfus in the early 5th century following the saint's appearance in a vision. It was sacked 100 years later by Saxon raiders, who eventually settled the area and began farming the slopes above the town, beginning the cultivation terraces known as lychets on Abbotsbury Plains. After the Saxons came the Vikings, who in turn established rule under King Cnut (Canute). Cnut gave Abbotsbury to his trusted steward Orc, who was a Christian and founded the abbey.

Although the abbey was largely demolished after the Dissolution, the Great Barn and St Catherine's Chapel were left alone. The barn served as a storehouse while the chapel's hilltop prominence made it a valuable navigation mark for ships. It is thought to have been built on an existing pagan site, and served as a retreat for the abbey's monks. St Catherine was the patron saint of unmarried girls, and later on the chapel attracted young maidens, who climbed the hill to pray for a husband.

The surrounding hills are rich in prehistoric remains. Just to the west is an impressive Iron Age site overlooking the English Channel and known as Abbotsbury Castle, while along the high ground of the ancient ridgeway are the mounds of numerous tumuli. On top of Tenants Hill beside the convergence of several paths is one of the walk's highlights, the Kingston Russell Stone Circle. Dated to the late Neolithic or early Bronze Age, it is around 4,000 years old and consists of 18 fallen stones in an irregular oval some 90ft by 60ft (27m by 18m). Tumuli and the earthworks of a settlement are scattered on the northern slope of the hill, while 0.5 miles (800m) to the southeast is another monument, perhaps 1,000 years older: the remains of a chambered long barrow known as The Grey Mare and her Colts.

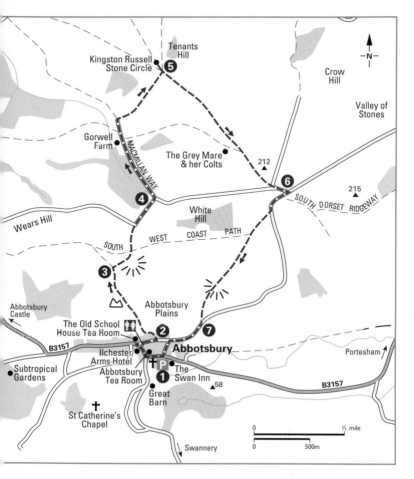

1. Leave the car park entrance and go left along the road, keeping with it as it bends right through the village. On reaching the Ilchester Arms Hotel, go right again past The Old School House Tea Room and public toilets.

2. After 150yds (137m), leave up Blind Lane, a track on the left signed to 'Hillfort and Hardy Monument'. Swinging left behind cottages and then right, it climbs steadily on to White Hill above the town. Through a gate at the top, carry on at the edge of scrub, passing a signpost to a gate higher up. Keep ahead over a grass bank towards a limestone outcrop, aiming for a field gate that comes into view.

3. Through that, bear right following a sign for the Hardy Monument. The way slants up between grassy hummocks, passing through another gate (the left of two field gates) and on by the left fence over the crest of the hill. Beyond a gate in the corner, go right through a smaller gate to descend along a contained track. Joining a concrete farm track, continue down to a farm lane along the wooded valley.

4. Follow it left to Gorwell Farm, passing between the buildings. Immediately after a gate below Mead Cottage at the far end, abandon the track and climb

151

right beside the boundary to the top right-hand corner. Go through the gate ahead and walk beside the right hedge, continuing in a second field to emerge onto a track running along the top of the hill. The onward route lies to the right, but first go into the field opposite to have a look at the Kingston Russell Stone Circle.

5. Return to the track and follow it southeast for 0.75 miles (1.2km). Eventually merging with another track, keep ahead to a metalled farm track and go left out to a lane.

6. Follow it right, going ahead at the next bend through a gate along a climbing field track. Abandon it on a bend at the crest through a gate on the left, bearing half right following the sign to Abbotsbury. Towards the far side of the field, the town comes into view and a developing grass track guides you down to a gate. A few paces later, fork left to follow the hollowed out track. Carry on, cutting across ancient ploughing terraces. Ignore a path signed off left and continue down to exit through a final gate onto a lane.

7. Turn right back to Abbotsbury, passing houses before forking left along Rosemary Lane, which returns you to the main street opposite the car park.

Where to eat and drink

There are several options in the village. The Swan Inn is a family pub with outside seating, while the Ilchester Arms Hotel is a former 17th-century coaching inn. Alternatively, try the Abbotsbury or The Old School House tea rooms. Both have a garden and serve light lunches and afternoon teas with home-made cakes and scones.

What to see

As you climb onto Abbotsbury Plains, above the village, look for veins of iron ore in the rock beside the track. It was hoped that the exploitation of these deposits would help justify the extension of the railway to Abbotsbury. Although the line arrived, in the end the industry never developed and the service merely carried local passengers and holiday traffic until its closure in 1952.

While you're there

Although little is left of the abbey, its remains together with the tithe barn can be seen as you follow the lane towards the Swannery. The climb to St Catherine's Chapel is also rewarding for the view. If you're interested in horticulture, pop along to the Subtropical Gardens, established in 1765. Spread over 30 acres (12ha), it contains rare and exotic plants from across the world.

ALONG THE FLEET BY CHESIL BEACH

DISTANCE/TIME	6 miles (9.7km) / 2hrs 30min
ASCENT/GRADIENT	430ft (131m) / ▲
PATHS	Coastal path (slippery after rain), country lanes
LANDSCAPE	Low hills and secretive villages inland from Chesil Beach
SUGGESTED MAP	AA Walker's Map 5 Weymouth & South Dorset
START/FINISH	Grid reference: SY633805
DOG FRIENDLINESS	Keep under close control around wildlife – particularly the numerous deer between Langton Herring and Gore Cove – and beware of racehorses training
PARKING	At the pinkish stone New Church, Fleet Common
PUBLIC TOILETS	None on route

Chesil Beach stretches 17 miles (27km) from Bridport's West Bay down to the cliffs at Portland. It's a unique feature, built by 'longshore drift'. Waves coming up the English Channel strike the shore at an angle, nudging beach pebbles eastwards. Over tens of thousands of years, this can transport stones right along the south coast, and Chesil pebbles derive from the cliffs of east Devon. Today it's estimated that Chesil Beach is still moving eastwards, up to 6 inches (15cm) a year. Wave action has also graded the stones by size, from hefty cobbles at the Portland end, down to pea-sized gravel at the western end. It is said that shipwrecked fishermen, or smugglers landing their booty in the dark, could tell their exact whereabouts by the size of the pebbles beneath their feet.

As striking is the seawater lagoon trapped behind the beach. The Fleet is some 8 miles (13km) long, and the still, muddy shallows benefit from vast underwater pastures of long, wavy eelgrass – great food for birds, and habitat for a variety of other marine life, even in winter. There's something eerie about the Fleet lagoon, trapped by its high bank of sighing golden shingle, its waters wave-free even on the stormy days. *On Chesil Beach* (2007) is Ian McEwan's grim little novel about a young couple failing to consummate their wedding night at a hotel not unlike Moonfleet Manor. A century earlier, John Meade Falkner captured the romantic atmosphere in *Moonfleet*, his 1898 adventure novel about smugglers and kidnapping. One of the beach's nicknames is Dead Man's Bay, a gruesome reflection of the many lives that have been lost in shipwrecks here, for on the seaward side of the bank the water is deep and treacherous. The village of East Fleet was the scene of dreadful destruction in 1824, when a violent storm swept the sea over the top of Chesil Bank and broke it open. The village was washed away, leaving nothing but the chancel of the church. That ruin still exists, containing memorials to the Mohun family. A few houses were rebuilt around it, but the main village now stands further inland.

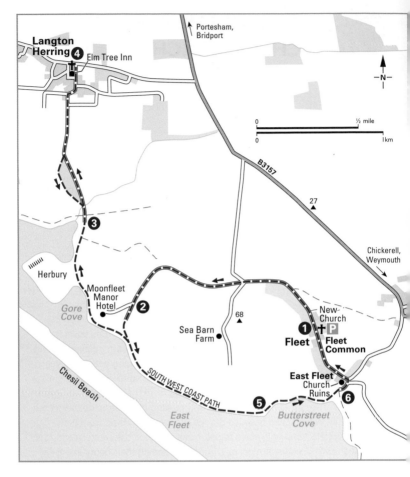

1. Continue up the road for 0.5 miles (800m) to a junction. Go straight ahead, passing a Victorian postbox on your left, through the manorial gateway with its stone lions. The sea now comes into view. Follow the road down through woods and past several houses. Before the road bends right over a stream to the Moonfleet Manor Hotel, take a gate on the left, signed 'To Coast Path'.

2. Walk down the field towards the Fleet, passing the Moonfleet Manor Hotel on your right. Bear left through a kissing gate and continue down. Turn right through a gate signposted 'Abbotsbury', joining the coastal path (which is marked with acorn motifs). Descend steps into some trees to cross a plank bridge. Continue below the hotel, passing an information board. The coast path passes around Gore Cove, then crosses a neck of land.

3. At the head of the next bay, after ignoring one footpath junction on the right, keep ahead on the second one, signposted 'Langton Herring'. Join a track uphill, with woodland on your left – on the return leg, you can pass around the seaward side of this wood. Beyond it, keep ahead to the edge of Langton Herring. Go through a gate, and bear right to reach Fleet Way Cottage. Turn right along the lane, which bends left to the Elm Tree pub.

4. Retrace your route to the sea, passing below the Moonfleet Manor Hotel again, and this time turn right along the fence on the green track of the South West Coast Path. After a gate, beware of passing racehorses from Sea Barn Farm, which train on the gallop beside you. You pass some old pill boxes, part of the massive fortification of the coast during World War II. The 'bouncing bomb' (of Dambusters fame) was tested in great secrecy on the Fleet during that period.

5. The path curves in round Butterstreet Cove. Keep right, down through wind-blown blackthorn and hawthorn. Cross a footbridge and go through a gate. After the next gate, turn inland beside a stream, towards the hamlet of East Fleet.

6. Bear right over the stream and immediately go left around what remains of the church. Go through a gate and straight ahead, past a row of cottages, to the road. Turn left and follow it uphill into the village of Fleet Common and the New Church.

Where to eat and drink

Moonfleet Manor Hotel is a haven of old-world charm and polished parquet floors. Dogs are welcome in the lounge bar (on leads) and on the terrace, both good places for lunch or afternoon tea. At Langton Herring the Elm Tree Inn welcomes walkers.

What to see

Mute swans are the most famous inhabitants of the Fleet, but there are other interesting birds to identify on these sheltered waters. Little terns migrate here from Africa to breed and nest along the gravel shore in April. Ringed plovers also nest on the beach. Geese fly in to over-winter here, notably Brent geese from Siberia. Red-breasted mergansers, widgeon and shelduck are other foreign migrants.

While you're there

You can see live pictures of the Fleet, relayed by underwater cameras, at the Chesil Beach Centre between Weymouth and Portland.

LULWORTH AND DURDLE DOOR

DISTANCE/TIME	6.75 miles (10.9km) / 3hrs
ASCENT/GRADIENT	1,247ft (380m) / ▲ ▲ ▲
PATHS	Stone path, grassy tracks, tarmac, muddy field path
LANDSCAPE	Steeply rolling cliffs beside sea, green inland
SUGGESTED MAP	AA Walker's Map 5 Weymouth & South Dorset
START/FINISH	Grid reference: SY821800
DOG FRIENDLINESS	Excitable dogs need strict control near cliff edge; the extension is not suitable for dogs
PARKING	Pay-and-display car park (busy), signed at Lulworth Cove
PUBLIC TOILETS	By Visitor Centre; on lane to Lulworth Cove; also at Newlands Farm caravan park
NOTES	The very steep descent of Bindon Hill extension is not for vertigo sufferers

Lulworth Cove is an almost circular bay in the rolling line of cliffs that form Dorset's southern coast. The cliffs around the eastern side of the bay are crumbly and brightly coloured in places, while beyond the opposite arm, at Stair Hole, the rock is folded. The intriguing geology earned Lulworth Cove World Heritage status in 2002. The oldest layer, easily identified here, is the gleaming white Portland stone. This was much employed by Christopher Wren in his rebuilding of London. It is a fine-grained oolite, around 140 million years old. It holds tightly compressed, fossilised shells – the flat-coiled ones are ammonites, while the long curly ones are a gastropod (snail) known as the Portland Screw. Occasional giant ammonites, called titanites, are incorporated into house walls across Purbeck.

As seen at Bat's Head, the rock may contain speckled bands of flinty chert. Above this is a layer of Purbeck marble, a limestone in which fossils are occasionally found. The soft layer above is the Wealden beds, a belt of colourful clays, silts and sands that are unstable and prone to landslips when exposed. Crumbly, white chalk overlays the Wealden beds. The chalk consists of the remains of microscopic sea creatures and shells deposited when sea covered much of Dorset, some 75 million years ago. This is the chalk that underlies Dorset's famous downland and is seen in the exposed cliffs at White Nothe. Hard nodules and bands of flint appear in the chalk, and in its gravel-beach form the flint protects long stretches of this fragile coast. The laying down of chalk marks the end of the Cretaceous period. After this the blanket of chalk was uplifted, folded and subjected to erosion by the movement of tectonic plates. The Dorset coast was exposed to extreme pressure during the rising of the Alps (still going on). The resulting folding and overturning of strata can be seen at Durdle Door, and as the 'Lulworth Crumple' at Stair Hole.

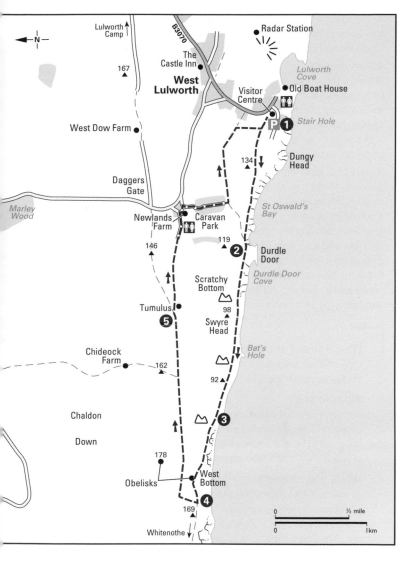

1. From the gate at the top of the car park take the broad, paved footpath up shallow steps to the top of the first hill. Continue along the brow, and down the other side, to pass below a caravan park. At a gate, turn left to Durdle Door.

2. Reach a cove enclosed from the sea by a line of rocks. At the time of writing, the steps that lead down to the sea here have been dismantled. Carry on ahead on the coast path, and the natural stone arch is revealed in Durdle Door Cove below you. The mass of Swyre Head looms close and, yes, that is the path you're going to take, straight up the side. The coast path descends a little, then climbs up to Swyre Head. The path leads steeply down again on the other side, to a cove with a sea stack and a small arch (Bat's Hole) on the right. Climb the next steep hill. Descend along the path just behind the cliffs, where the land tilts away from the sea.

3. The path climbs more gently up the next hill. After a navigation obelisk (the lower of two), the path curves gently to the left for 0.25 miles (400m) round the contour above West Bottom.

4. Turn right, through a metal kissing gate, on a side path with a marker stone for Daggers Gate. Head inland, with a fence on your left. The path curves round so you're walking parallel with the coast on level greensward. Pass three stone embrasures, two of them with shell sculptures, with the upper obelisk over on your left. Keep straight ahead along the tops of the fields, until the path descends gently to a narrow gate, a wider one alongside, and a roundel bearing the words 'Walk 6 – Permissive Path'.

5. Here bear half right, out into the field. After 150yds (140m) pass to left of a tumulus. Ahead is a narrow gate at the bottom corner of a field, but only go through this to read the interpretation board just above. Otherwise stay below a belt of gorse bushes, to walk above the hollow called Scratchy Bottom. A gate leads into a green lane to Newlands Farm. Follow the driveway round to the right, and turn right into the caravan park. Go straight down the road through here. At the far side go through a gate on the left, signed to West Lulworth. Stay along the field-edge, down a little valley then bending right above a farm, and around the end of the hill. Keep straight on at the fingerpost and reach the gate above the car park.

Where to eat and drink
Lulworth has several tea rooms, hotel restaurants and cafés, including the highly-rated Boat Shed Café near the shore.

What to see
Don't miss the baby-blue-painted Dolls House on the way down to Lulworth Cove. It's a fisherman's cottage dating from 1861; 11 children were raised here. It's now a sweet shop, which is doubtless something of which they would have approved.

While you're there
At nearby East Lulworth is Lulworth Castle Park. The castle itself, a 17th-century hunting lodge built four-square with pepperpot towers, is a handsome shell, but was gutted by fire in 1929 and only partly restored. Other attractions on the estate include a circular chapel, an animal farm, an adventure playground for children and a tea room.

FROM KIMMERIDGE TO TYNEHAM

DISTANCE/TIME	7.5 miles (12.1km) / 3hrs 30min
ASCENT/GRADIENT	1,165ft (355m) / ▲ ▲ ▲
PATHS	Grassy tracks and bridle paths, some road walking
LANDSCAPE	Folded hills and valleys around Kimmeridge Bay
SUGGESTED MAP	AA Walker's Map 5 Weymouth & South Dorset
START/FINISH	Grid reference: SY918800
DOG FRIENDLINESS	Notices request dogs on leads in some sections; some road walking
PARKING	Car park (free) in old quarry north of Kimmeridge village
PUBLIC TOILETS	Near Wild Seas Centre at Kimmeridge Bay and Tyneham
NOTES	Range walks open most weekends throughout year and during main holiday periods; see dorsetforyou.com for further information; keep strictly to paths, between yellow-marked posts

There's a bleakness about Kimmeridge Bay. Giant slabs of black rock shelving out to sea, with crumbling cliffs topped by clumps of wild cabbage, create something of this mood. The slight smell of paraffin from the oil shales and the slow, steady movement of the nodding donkey of the oil well above a little terrace of unmistakably industrial cottages reinforce it.

The story of the bay is intriguing. Iron Age tribes spotted the potential of the band of bituminous shale that runs through Kimmeridge, polishing it up into blackstone arm rings and ornaments, and later into chair and table legs. People have been trying to exploit it ever since. The shale, permeated with crude oil, is also known as Kimmeridge coal, but successive attempts to work it on an industrial scale seemed doomed to failure. These included alum extraction (for dyeing) in the 16th century; use of the coal to fuel a glassworks in the 17th century (it was smelly and inefficient); and use for a variety of chemical distillations, including paraffin wax and varnish, in the 19th century. And, for one brief period, the street lights of Paris were lit by gas extracted from the shale oil. However, nothing lasted very long. Since 1959 BP has drilled down 1,716ft (520m) below the sea, and its beam engine sucks out some 80 barrels (2,800 gallons/12,720 litres) of crude oil a day. Transported to the Wytch Farm collection point (near Corfe Castle), the oil is then pumped to Hamble, to be shipped around the world.

In contrast to Kimmeridge, Tyneham is a cosy farming village clustered around its church in a glorious valley. As you get up close, however, you realise that it's uncannily neat, like a film set from the 1940s – Greer Garson's Mrs Miniver could appear at any moment. There's a spreading oak tree by the church gate; a quaint old phone box; even a village pump. The gravestones all look freshly scrubbed – no lichen here. The farmyard is swept clean and empty. The stone cottages are newly repointed, but roofless. And the church, as you enter on a chill midwinter day, is warm! Inside is an exhibition to explain all. The villagers were asked to give up their homes in December 1943 for the 'war effort', and Tyneham became absorbed into the vast Lulworth Ranges, as part of the live firing range. It's a touching memorial, though nothing can make up for the fact that the villagers were never allowed back to their homes.

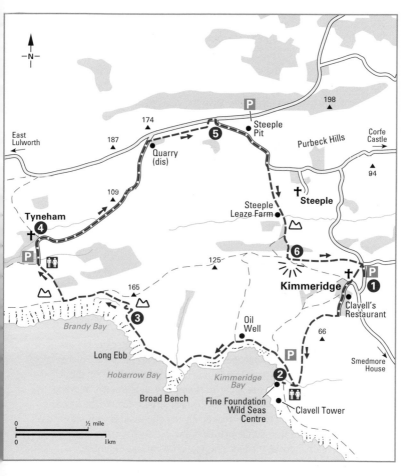

1. Turn right up the road and soon left over a stile, signposted 'Kimmeridge' – enjoy the sweeping views as you descend. Go through two gates passing the church, then on down the road. After the last house, a path on the right runs alongside the road, then rejoins it before the gate marking where it becomes a private toll road. Follow this on around the hillside and, where it forks, keep ahead, marked 'Boats and Slipway'. At a stream, your onward route turns right through a car park with toilets but first, you could continue ahead to visit the Wild Seas Centre (open Easter to October).

2. Cross the foot of the car park with the toilets (signed 'Range Walks'). Cross the foot of another car park, then descend some steps, cross a bridge and bear right (down left is to the beach). Pass to the left of some cottages and then the oil well. Go through the gate onto the range walk and continue around the coast on a track between yellow posts, crossing two cattle grids. The cliffs of Brandy Bay stagger away to the west.

3. After a mile (1.6km) cross a stile by a gate and follow the path as it zig-zags sharply uphill. Turn left at the top along a very narrow path to join the coast path at a gate. Continue around the top of Brandy Bay on the cliff path. When you reach a stile and marker stone turn down to the right, signposted 'Tyneham'. Soon go through a gate to the left and follow the track down into Tyneham village.

4. After exploring, take the exit road all the way up the hill. At the top, turn right along a path immediately below the road.

5. Emerge at a gate and turn right down the road, to go past Steeple Pit. Where the road turns sharp left, go straight ahead on the tarmac drive through Steeple Leaze Farm and, heading over a stream, take the stony track ahead, leading straight up the hill under trees. After a gate, keep left up a muddy path that winds through gorse and scrub up the hill. Go through a gateway at the top and continue straight ahead, climbing to a viewpoint over Kimmeridge.

6. Turn left in front of a gate, and go straight along the edge of the field, following the ridge of the hill, for 0.5 miles (800m), with views to Smedmore House and Corfe Castle. At the road turn right to return to the start.

Where to eat and drink

Clavell's Restaurant in the former post office at Kimmeridge serves cream teas, locally sourced meat and seafood. Dogs are welcome in the large outdoor seating area.

What to see

Kimmeridge's unique combination of clear, shallow water, double low tides and accessible rocky ledges make it the ideal choice for a pioneering underwater nature reserve. The double low tide is at its best in the afternoons – effectively, the water may stay low all afternoon, allowing optimum access to the fingers of rock which stretch out into the bay. The low water uncovers a world of rockpools and gullies alive with seaweeds, anemones and creatures that include crabs, blennies and the bizarre pipefish. Learn more at the Fine Foundation Wild Seas Centre.

While you're there

The Clavell family have been at Smedmore since the 13th century. In 1575 John Clavell was attempting to exploit the Kimmeridge shale for alum (an essential ingredient for the dyeing industry), and the current Smedmore House, a handsome twin-bayed affair dating from 1761, still keeps a firm eye on activities in the bay. The house is open in high summer, when you can enjoy its attractive gardens, the rococo details, period furniture and a museum collection of dolls.

WORTH MATRAVERS
TO CORFE CASTLE

DISTANCE/TIME	9 miles (14.5km) / 3hrs 45min
ASCENT/GRADIENT	1,083ft (330m) / ▲ ▲ ▲
PATHS	Village lanes, rocky lanes (slippery after rain), moorland tracks, grassy paths, steep cliff path with steps
LANDSCAPE	Fields and tracks, path, coastal path
SUGGESTED MAP	AA Walker's Map 5 Weymouth & South Dorset
START/FINISH	Grid reference: SY974776
DOG FRIENDLINESS	Good, though some stiles challenging. On lead in Worth Matravers (free-range poultry) and in pasture around Corfe and Kingston
PARKING	Car park just north of Worth Matravers (honesty box)
PUBLIC TOILETS	At car park; also Corfe Castle by car park

Worth Matravers is a picturesque village of lichen-encrusted grey cottages. Men from here have worked the nearby quarries for centuries, and local stone was used to build Salisbury Cathedral. By contrast, the huge and toothy ruin of Corfe Castle seems to fill the gap in the wall of the Purbeck Hills with its presence. It stands on a high mound, and must have been massively imposing when whole. The castle has a grim history. In AD 978 a youthful King Edward (the Martyr) was murdered here while visiting his stepmother, Elfthryth. His body was buried without ceremony at Wareham, while his half-brother took the throne as Ethelred II. However, stories of miracles occurring soon resulted in Edward's body being exhumed and transported to Shaftesbury, where an abbey grew up in his honour. His sacred relics were recovered in 1931 and reburied, incredibly, in Brookwood Cemetery, to the west of London.

The Normans realised the commanding role a castle could play in defence at Corfe, and built the big square keep around 1106. King John starved 22 French noblemen to death in the dungeons here in 1204 and used it as a lifelong prison for his niece Eleanor, a potential threat to his throne. The unfortunate Edward II, deposed by his wife Isabella and her favourite, Roger de Mortimer, was also imprisoned here briefly. The castle again came to the fore during the Civil War. Its owner, Sir John Bankes, having sought and failed to make peace between factions, sided with the King. However, it was his spirited wife Mary who was left, with a handful of women and just five men, to fight off a siege in 1642, when a 500-strong Parliamentarian army reached Corfe Castle. Despite reinforcements, they failed to take the castle. After a second, more sustained siege, the castle was betrayed in 1646 by one of its defenders and Lady Bankes was forced to give it up. The castle was slighted to prevent its further use. Close up, the sagging towers of the gatehouse and the crazy angle of the outer walls give the impression they were blown up only days ago.

163

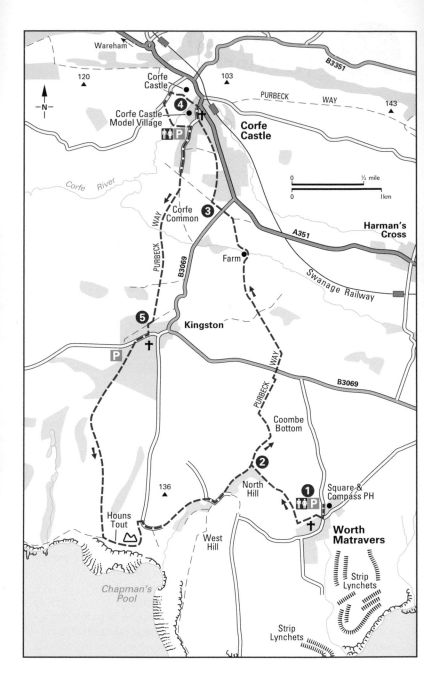

1. Turn down the street for 80yds (75m) then right, up a path by a fingerpost signed 'Hill Bottom'. Turn left through the first of three gates, walking behind the village. Turn right at another fingerpost ('Hill Bottom'), up to cross the wall and continue down the next field. At the bottom bear left over the stile, walking down a narrow cutting to cross a stile at its foot.

2. Turn right on the Purbeck Way. Ignore a left fork to continue on the main track. The path runs up the valley, bending left as the valley divides. It turns right, then gently uphill (north). Go through the gateway at the top, ahead on a track. Go through a field gate to pass to the left of a farm to the road. Cross into the track opposite, signed 'Purbeck Way'. As the track bends right, take the second path on the left, passing through a kissing gate. Continue down the left edges of three fields, left across a footbridge and back right. Pass through a gate, a copse and another gate, cross a boardwalk and two footbridges. Bear half left at a fingerpost ('Corfe Castle') to cross a further footbridge. Stay left as a wider grassy path comes in from the right and walk to the road.

3. Cross to a track on the other side. Bear round to the right behind houses to a gate. Follow the path towards the village centre. Head along a cul-de-sac, cross a road and head along an alleyway. Turn right, through a gate, and cross fields into a playground. Turn left, then right into West Street to the square.

4. At the castle entrance turn left on the path below the walls. Go left up the road and in 160yds (150m) left again through a kissing gate into fields. Cross them (southeast) over a pair of footbridges, to a car park. Bear right, then right again into West Street. At its end, go straight on over a cattle grid. Bear left (south) on a path across the heath with a view of Kingston and its church up ahead. Cross duckboards and go uphill, bearing right off the main path at a National Trust post signed 'Kingston'. Turn right at a T-junction then take the first left to cross the crest to the right of a stone block. Following another NT signpost ('Kingston' again), head down to a hidden gate. After two footbridges, slant up and left to a hedge gap, then carry on over the next field to a gate, footbridge and duckboards beside the stream. Continue straight uphill, emerging from woods into a field. Carry on uphill, over two stiles as you cross a track. Above the next field, join an earth track below Kingston's first houses.

5. Take the earth track up to the right. Immediately after a track junction, turn left, up through trees, then left at the top to a road. Turn right, soon taking the track on the left, signed 'Houns Tout'. Follow this for 1.5 miles (2.5km) to the sea, and left along cliff tops. Descend steps, then cross a stile at the bottom. Head inland to a road. Turn right and follow it to its end, bearing left on a track signed 'Coast Path'. Beside Hill Bottom Cottage bear right. Carry on for 150yds (140m) until the road swings right, and turn left up Hill Bottom. After 0.25 miles (400m) turn right over a stile; retrace your steps to the car park.

Where to eat and drink
In the Square and Compass in Worth Matravers they serve pasties with a range of real ales and home-pressed ciders. Dogs are welcome.

What to see
Towards the end of the walk, as you descend from Houns Tout towards Chapman's Pool, keep your eyes peeled for adders.

While you're there
Visit Corfe Castle Model Village, open daily from Easter to the end of October.

ST ALDHELM'S HEAD AND WORTH MATRAVERS

48

DISTANCE/TIME	5 miles (8km) / 2hrs 15min
ASCENT/GRADIENT	980ft (299m) / ▲ ▲ ▲
PATHS	Field and coastal cliff paths, some long and steep gradients
LANDSCAPE	Coastal downland
SUGGESTED MAP	AA Walker's Map 5 Weymouth & South Dorset
START/FINISH	Grid reference: SY974776
DOG FRIENDLINESS	Under close control above cliffs and on leads near grazing livestock
PARKING	Car park just north of Worth Matravers (honesty box)
PUBLIC TOILETS	At car park

In 1866, a lifeboat station was established in the shelter of Chapman's Pool but, plagued by constant landslip, difficult to launch against a southwesterly gale and too remote to be effectively manned, it was abandoned after only 15 years. The coastguard was originally stationed there too, but relocated to St Aldhelm's Head in 1895, with a row of cottages built for the crew. The visual lookout dates from the 1970s, but has been manned since the mid-1990s by volunteers of the National Coastwatch Institution.

The origin of the nearby chapel is lost in time and, because it is not aligned to the east and has no altar, some doubt that it was built as such. Although the roof, supported by vaulting springing from a central column, now bears a cross on its pinnacle, there is evidence that it originally supported a beacon to warn shipping. Nevertheless, there was a priest during the 13th century, when it served as a chantry to offer prayers for lost sailors, and a local legend tells that it was built by a grieving father, after his daughter and her husband were drowned when their boat capsized in a storm.

During World War II, the headland was the site of a radar research station, which developed the rotating aerial and plan position indicator to plot moving targets. As the threat of enemy raids increased, the boffins were moved to Malvern in 1942, but the radar remained with the establishment of a Chain Home station to provide early warning of bombing raids. After the war, the station continued as an RAF training establishment, with the last of the radar towers only being dismantled in the 1970s. Just north, on the edge of Emmetts Hill, is a memorial garden to Royal Marines killed in service since 1945. It was established by members of the Royal Marines Association following the IRA attack on the Marines' barracks at Deal in 1989, and overlooks an area that the service has often used for training.

The cliffs below St Aldhelm's were heavily quarried for Portland stone. The Victorian quarrymen have left an impressive monolith, a common practice to indicate how much stone had been removed. Further east at Winspit are more quarries. Here the quarrymen tunnelled into the cliffs. Work stopped during World War II and the caves were used by the military. Today they are home to bats, including the rare greater horseshoe bat, one of Britain's largest species. The site has been used as a film location for both *Blake's 7* and *Doctor Who*.

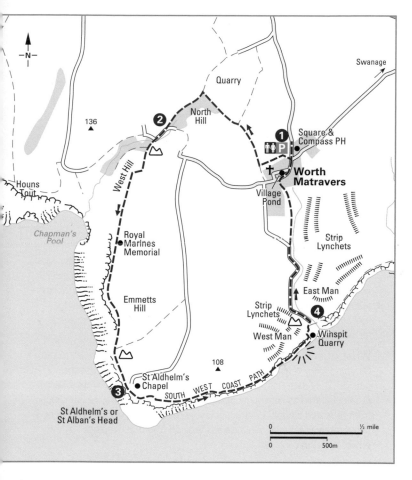

1. Leaving the car park, turn down towards the village. However, just after reaching the Square and Compass, turn off right on a path signed to Hill Bottom and Chapman's Pool. Pass behind a cottage and through a gate to walk across a paddock, and then at the edge of a couple of fields to meet another path from the village. Turn right and continue over a stile along the edge of the next field. Exit the corner and follow a broad path down a curving gully below embanked quarry workings. Meeting a crossing track, go left, eventually dropping down left to a narrow lane and following it right for 100yds (91m).

2. Bear off left by a coast path sign, passing over a bridge and through a gate. Immediately fork left to climb a steep grass path across the valley side. Broaching the top, a superb view opens across Chapman's Pool. The path now runs easily along the valley rim towards the coast, passing a small

memorial garden dedicated to Royal Marines killed in action. Continue at the edge of Emmetts Hill above the cliffs, making for St Aldhelm's Head, whose buildings now appear in the distance. However before reaching them, the path descends abruptly down a long flight of steps into a deep valley, climbing out just as uncompromisingly up the other side.

3. Have a look in the tiny stone chapel over to the left, then return to the National Coastwatch lookout to continue above the cliffs. After passing above the abandoned St Aldhelm's quarry, fork right with the coast path, losing height to undulate above lower cliffs. Approaching the snout of West Man, the path rises behind the old Winspit workings before descending steps into a valley.

4. At the bottom follow a track from the coast towards Worth Matravers, which rises steadily along the valley base. Reaching a fork, branch right onto a gravel path; it leads up into open pasture. Bear left, climbing across the hillside towards Worth Matravers. Exiting through a gate at the top, carry on along a path and then a short street into the village. Go right to the main lane and right again, finally turning left past the Square and Compass to the car park.

Where to eat and drink

The Square and Compass has been an alehouse since 1776. A lively local pub, it is open all day during the summer, serving traditional cider and local beers with its famous home-made pies and pasties. The Worth Matravers Tea & Supper Room has a secluded garden and is open for lunches and delicious cream teas Wednesday to Sunday, with bookings for evening meals taken on Saturday.

What to see

Climbing from Winspit along the valley, look for lynchets across the hillside. They date from at least the 13th century, when the slopes were strip-cultivated as communal open fields. The terraces may result simply from repeated ploughing, although some researchers believe they were deliberately created to minimise soil erosion. The practice ended at the end of the 18th century.

While you're there

The Square and Compass has a small museum of local curios that includes a surprising assortment of fossils with an almost complete example of an ichthyosaur. There are archaeological artefacts spanning the Stone Age to the coming of the Romans and a miscellany of farming implements including such indispensable tools as a cow cake cutter.

EXPLORING SWANAGE

DISTANCE/TIME	4.25 miles (6.8km) / 2hrs 30min
ASCENT/GRADIENT	509ft (155m) / ▲ ▲ ▲
PATHS	Grassy paths, rocky tracks, pavements
LANDSCAPE	Spectacular cliff scenery, undulating hills, Swanage town
SUGGESTED MAP	AA Walker's Map 5 Weymouth & South Dorset
START/FINISH	Grid reference: SZ031773
DOG FRIENDLINESS	Some town walking
PARKING	Durlston Country Park (pay and display)
PUBLIC TOILETS	Durlston Country Park; Peveril Point

In the early 19th century Swanage was a bustling, industrial port that shipped stone from the 60 or so quarries in the area. A growing fashion for seabathing changed the focus of the town forever. The real change to the face of Swanage came, however, with the extraordinary collecting habit of George Burt, a contractor with an eye for architecture. With his uncle, John Mowlem, a local stonemason and philanthropist, Burt shipped marble from the quarries of Purbeck to London, where old buildings were being knocked down for a wave of new construction. Reluctant to see such splendid stonework discarded, Burt salvaged whole pieces, transported them back in the company ships, and re-erected them in Swanage, giving it an instant architectural heritage.

The first you see of Burt's influence is as you walk past the Town Hall. Burt had donated a plain and simple building to the town in 1872, but in 1883 he added a façade by Sir Christopher Wren, appropriately in Portland stone, which he had rescued from the front of the Mercers' Hall in London's Cheapside. Architectural commentator Sir Nikolaus Pevsner described its florid carvings of stone fruit and wreaths as 'overwhelmingly undisciplined'. Next, in the park near the pier, are a grand archway removed from Hyde Park Corner, three statues and some columns rescued from Billingsgate Market. There's also an absurd but rather elegant clock tower, removed from the south end of London Bridge in 1867, where it had been set as a memorial to the Duke of Wellington.

Durlston Castle is an original folly by Burt dating from 1887, designed from the start as a clifftop restaurant on Durlston Head. It has an unexpected educational element, as facts and figures from around the world are carved into great stone slabs set into the walls below. Burt added a large, segmented stone globe of the world, but it's rather grey and a little disappointing. Finally, Burt was also influential in bringing the railway to Swanage in 1885 – this gave major impetus to the development of the town as a seaside resort. The railway closed in the early 1960s, but was revived by enthusiasts who, early in 2002, achieved their ambition of linking back up to the main line station at Wareham. Today it transports visitors on a nostalgic trip between Swanage and Corfe Castle.

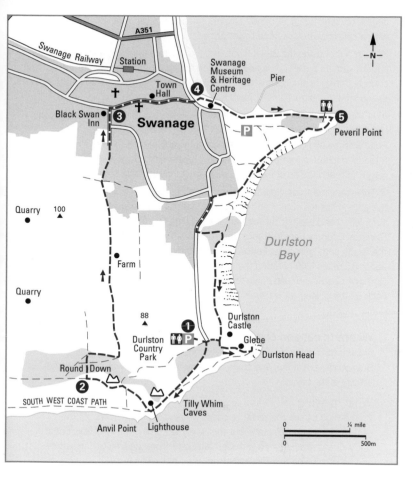

1. From the top of the main path down to the castle from the car park, turn right along a tarmac footpath. In 75yds (70m), find steps and an earth path down through trees. Cross a path and, with the sea ahead of you, follow the way round downhill to the right, towards the lighthouse. As you climb up the other side, look back to admire the Tilly Whim Caves cut into the ledges of the cliff. Immediately after the lighthouse turn up right towards the hump of Round Down. Don't join the tarmac path down to the right, but instead head left, skirting to the right of a thorn patch to a kissing gate with a butterfly marker. A path with small waymarkers leads from here up onto the down.

2. Don't go through the wall at the top, but turn down right parallel to it into a little valley. At the bottom, go through a gate and cross a little footbridge and turn right on a grassy track slanting up to a wooden gate. Just before this gate, turn left through another gate (stone stile alongside). A wide green path leads inland, gently uphill. After another gate you can see the Purbeck Hills ahead and the roofs of Swanage to the right. The path goes down through another gate to join a broad, grassy track. After passing a farm, this track narrows and

begins to climb again. Continue straight ahead onto the road into the town, with a church with low stone tower ahead.

3. Turn right beside the Black Swan Inn. It's worth pausing to admire the little square with its butter cross and old stone houses tumbling down to the church. Continue along the street, but look out for No. 82A, home of Taffy Evans, and the extraordinary Town Hall with its Wren frontage.

4. At the Square bear left beside the Heritage Centre, to the seafront. Turn right and pass the entrance to the pier. Follow the blue signpost ('Peveril Point') below two Greek columns, to join a tarmac path with SWCP markers. It leads to a lane passing above a modern apartment block and a bizarre stone tower, to reach the tip of Peveril Point, with its coastguard station.

5. Turn back right and walk up the grassy slope along the top of the cliffs. Take the path in the top corner and follow the Victoria's head waymarker to a road. Turn left, then keep left through an area of pleasant Victorian villas. Near the Durlston Country Park entrance, turn down left into woodland, signposted to the castle and lighthouse. Follow the path down through the woods, then for about 0.5 miles (800m) along the cliff top to Durlston Head. Pass above Durlston Castle and turn down to examine Burt's great stone globe. Stagger back up the geological walkway to the car park.

Where to eat and drink
At Durlston Castle, the Seventh Wave café offers locally caught fish. But you can't beat fish and chips eaten by the harbour, watching the activity in the bay.

What to see
On the High Street, the small terraced house at No. 82A bears a 19th-century fire insurance plate, but this was the home of Petty Officer Edgar 'Taffy' Evans. He perished with Captain Scott from the effects of frostbite and exhaustion on the way back from the South Pole in 1912.

While you're there
Pop into Swanage Museum and Heritage Centre (closed in winter) and learn more about the area, including tales of smuggling and the development of the stone-quarrying industry. Pay a nominal fee and enjoy Swanage's Victorian pier – no seaside visit can be complete without it. The pier was restored for the Millennium with the help of the Lottery Heritage Fund but still needs to raise money for essential maintenance.

PORTLAND BILL
COASTAL TOUR

DISTANCE/TIME	3.5 miles (5.7km) / 1hr 30min
ASCENT/GRADIENT	165ft (50m) / ▲
PATHS	Stony and on grass, level or gently undulating, village road
LANDSCAPE	Grassy paths and tracks, level cliff tops, abandoned quarries
SUGGESTED MAP	AA Walker's Map 5 Weymouth & South Dorset
START/FINISH	Grid reference: SY688700
DOG FRIENDLINESS	Beware of unfenced cliff tops
PARKING	By roadside in centre of Southwell village, at road junction by Eight Kings pub
PUBLIC TOILETS	At Portland Bill near the main lighthouse

The great natural causeway of Chesil Beach joins the treeless peninsula known as the Isle of Portland. Described by Thomas Hardy as 'Dorset's Gibraltar', it is like nowhere else in Dorset. The rapid currents hereabouts are known as the Portland Race, and have claimed the lives of many seafarers.

You pass three lighthouses on this walk at Portland Bill. The Lower Lighthouse, just inland, is an RSPB bird observatory with accommodation – the Bill is a key point for watching cross-channel migrations. The second lighthouse is the largest and has a visitor centre. The third (the Higher Lighthouse), the smallest, is by the lookout station and is privately owned.

Here you are in the territory of Dorset's very own stone rush. Portland stone graces many of Britain's public buildings, among them the Tower of London, the British Museum and Buckingham Palace, as well as the United Nations building in New York. It was first quarried by the Romans. Some quarries are still worked today; others are abandoned. On this walk you'll see several of the winches once used for loading the stone onto boats.

Portland Stone was forming high façades and pinnacles long before Sir Christopher Wren specified it for St Paul's Cathedral. This tough limestone is responsible for sea cliff features all along the Dorset coast. Among these are the hard rocks forming the 'doorposts' at Lulworth Cove and the sea stacks in Mupe Bay, as well as Durdle Door. Around the Portland clifftops you can see the strikingly regular jointing of the rock that makes it so suitable for cutting and carving into cathedrals and palaces. Many of the loose blocks are crammed full of oyster-like fossils, betraying the limestone's origin on the floor of a warm, subtropical sea of the Jurassic period. At that time, about 140 million years ago, continental drift was carrying what we now call Britain across the Mediterranean, at the same time as an episode of global warming. The quarries yield monster ammonites the size of car tyres, and the occasional dinosaur. The small curly gastropod (snail) known as the Portland Screw is well displayed in the Portland Stone used for refacing the Cobb at Lyme Regis.

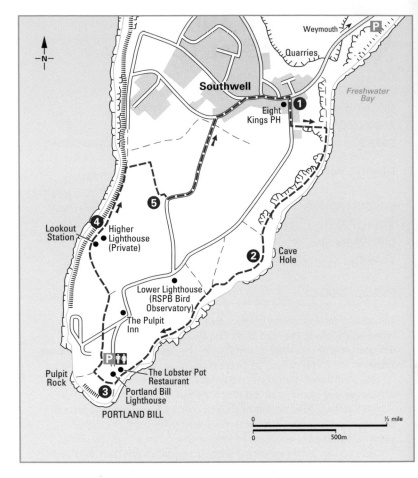

1. Follow the High Street, to the left of the Eight Kings pub, to the edge of the village, then turn left on a signposted path, just before the 40mph restriction roadsign. Turn right on the coastal path, which you'll then be following all the way to Portland Bill lighthouse. The path leads past old quarries, then along turf, crossing a footbridge. Soon look out for a deep hollow on your left, with iron rails across a great hole; this is Cave Hole, with a blowhole in the cliff top where the sea rushes into a cave below. You can sit on the big stone blocks and look down from there at this natural spectacle.

2. A huge collection of multicoloured sheds on the turf are Portland's answer to beach huts. The coast path goes through a gate with a Crown Estates sign. Just beyond here the sea rushes into an inlet and rebounds: you can see how it has cut out great scoops of the rock over the millennia. You also pass some sea stacks – pinnacles of wave-eroded rock. Reach the Lobster Pot restaurant near the Portland Bill car park. Keep to the left of the main lighthouse, turning right before a three-sided stone obelisk inscribed 'TH, 1844' erected as a landmark to aid shipping.